THE MUSIC LIBRARY

The History of Jazz

Stuart A. Kallen

LUCENT BOOKS

A part of Gale, Cengage Learning

GALE
CENGAGE Learning™

Detroit • New York • San Francisco • New Haven, Conn • Waterville, Maine • London

GALE
CENGAGE Learning·

LIBRARY OF CONGRESS CATALOGING-IN-PUBLICATION DATA

Kallen, Stuart A., 1955-
   The history of jazz / by Stuart A. Kallen.
     p. cm. -- (The music library)
   Includes bibliographical references and index.
   ISBN 978-1-4205-0820-8 (hardcover)
   1. Jazz--History and criticism--Juvenile literature. I. Title.
   ML3506.K35 2012
     781.6509--dc23   2012004927

Lucent Books
27500 Drake Rd.
Farmington Hills, MI 48331

ISBN-13: 978-1-4205-0820-8
ISBN-10: 1-4205-0820-2

Printed in the United States of America
1 2 3 4 5 6 7 16 15 14 13 12

CONTENTS

In the nineteenth century, English novelist Charles Kingsley wrote, "Music speaks straight to our hearts and spirits, to the very core and root of our souls. . . . Music soothes us, stirs us up . . . melts us to tears." As Kingsley stated, music is much more than just a pleasant arrangement of sounds. It is the resonance of emotion, a joyful noise, a human endeavor that can soothe the spirit or excite the soul. Musicians can also imitate the expressive palette of the earth, from the violent fury of a hurricane to the gentle flow of a babbling brook.

The word *music* is derived from the fabled Greek muses, the children of Apollo who ruled the realms of inspiration and imagination. Composers have long called upon the muses for help and insight. Music is not merely the result of emotions and pleasurable sensations, however.

Music is a discipline subject to formal study and analysis. It involves the juxtaposition of creative elements such as rhythm, melody, and harmony with intellectual aspects of composition, theory, and instrumentation. Like painters mixing red, blue, and yellow into thousands of colors, musicians blend these various elements to create classical symphonies, jazz improvisations, country ballads, and rock-and-roll tunes.

Throughout centuries of musical history, individual musical elements have been blended and modified in infinite ways. The resulting sounds may convey a whole range of moods, emotions, reactions, and messages. Music, then, is both an expression and reflection of human experience and emotion.

The foundations of modern musical styles were laid down by the first ancient musicians who used wood, rocks, animal skins—and their own bodies—to re-create the sounds of the natural world in which they lived. With their hands, their feet, and their very breath they ignited the passions of listeners and moved them to their feet. The dancing, in turn, had a mesmerizing and hypnotic effect that allowed people to transcend their worldly concerns. Through music they could achieve a level of shared experience that could not be found in other forms of communication. For this reason, music has always been part of religious endeavors, from ancient Egyptian spiritual ceremonies to modern Christian masses. And it has inspired dance movements from kings and queens spinning the minuet to punk rockers slamming together in a mosh pit.

By examining musical genres ranging from Western classical music to rock and roll, readers will find a new understanding of old music and develop an appreciation for new sounds. Books in Lucent's Music Library focus on the music, the musicians, the instruments, and on music's place in cultural history. The songs and artists examined may be easily found in the CD and sheet music collections of local libraries so that readers may study and enjoy the music covered in the books. Informative sidebars, annotated bibliographies, and complete indexes highlight the text in each volume and provide young readers with many opportunities for further discussion and research.

"Never Played the Same Way Once"

In 2011, Esperanza Spalding won the Grammy Award for Best New Artist for her album *Chamber Music Society*. The innovative twenty-six-year-old bass player was the first jazz musician to ever win the award in the fifty-three-year history of the Grammys. Spalding's musical roots stem from 1970s fusion, which mixes funk and rock rhythms with various forms of jazz.

Spalding's success was one of the bright spots for jazz music in recent history. The year before her Grammy win, only 8 million jazz records were sold, which was less than 2.5 percent of all record sales. This pales in comparison to 1928 when jazz music was the defining sound of the United States. More than 100 million jazz records were sold annually during the Roaring Twenties, nearly one record for every person living in the country at that time.

Record sales are only part of the modern jazz story. In the twenty-first century, jazz can be found at the roots of nearly every musical style. According to jazz authorities Joachim-Ernst Berendt and Günther Huesmann:

> [The] popular music of our time feeds on jazz: all the music we hear in TV series and elevators, in hotel lobbies and in ads, in movies and on MP3 players; all the music to which we dance, from the Charleston to rock, funk and hip-hop; all those sounds that daily engulf

us—all that music comes from jazz because their beats came . . . from jazz.[1]

Ragged Rhythms

Music based on jazz beats can be heard all over the world, but the roots of the style are distinctly American. Jazz grew out of the musical hothouse that was New Orleans, Louisiana, at the end of the nineteenth century. During that time, African American musicians blended several styles of music to create a completely new sound. These styles included work songs, spirituals, field hollers, blues, Mardi Gras marches, and European military music.

At first, the new music was called ragtime, possibly because of its "ragged" rhythms. By the 1910s, the sound was labeled jass or jazz. The origins of the word are unclear, but legend has it that jazz was used in New Orleans as a slang word for sex. The word was commonly used in the houses of prostitution that lined the streets of the notorious Storyville district where musicians played. Some historians believe, however, that the word may have originally meant "hurry up," and was first used by Afro-Caribbean musicians who instructed their bands to play faster by saying "Jass it up, boys!"[2]

Swinging and Jamming

Jazz music is defined by three main elements: swing, improvisation, and a distinctive voice. Swing is the driving rhythmic beat that makes people want to dance, clap along, or tap their feet. Jazz composer Duke Ellington immortalized this feeling in his song "It Don't Mean a Thing (If It Ain't Got That Swing)." Jazz artists can make music swing by accenting particular rhythms. Most early jazz was played in a steady repetitive beat, known as 4/4 time, because there are four beats to every measure. When the players hit a note a little before or slightly after the beat, the music has syncopation. When this happens, the music is described by players as "swinging," or having an "edge" or "groove."

Through the use of syncopation, musicians can create a variety of feelings. When playing slightly after the beat, musicians can get a laid-back or soulful sound. By playing before the beat, the music can sound exciting and put listeners on the edge of their seats or make them get up and dance. Another method for creating swing is called polyrhythm. This is the simultaneous playing of two or more independent rhythms, which gives the music a danceable, swinging momentum.

Jazz musicians also thrive on improvisation—that is, they create melodies on the spot rather than reading from previously written music scores. Improvised musical passages are called "riffs" or "licks" by musicians. The act of improvising is known as "jamming" or "ad-libbing." When jazz musicians jam, they take turns playing solos. This allows individual players in a group to show off their creativity and musical skills, or "chops." Jazz players believe an infinite number of melodies can be played within any song. As jazz legend Louis Armstrong once joked, "Jazz is music that's never played the same way once."[3]

Improvisers often imitate singing with their instruments—gliding, swooping, and soaring through seemingly endless cascades of notes. Musicians (especially horn players) create "blue" notes by bending or wavering between two different tones.

The best jazz players aspire to create a unique sound, or "voice." Individuals create a voice by varying tone, creatively selecting notes, and having a distinct sense of rhythm. Because of the individual voices possessed by jazz greats, most fans can identify the playing of Miles Davis or the saxophone riffs of Charlie Parker. The musician's voice is a product of his or her emotional state, which may move an audience through a cascade of emotions.

A Unifying Sound

Just as jazz reflects the wide-ranging emotions of the musicians, it also reflects the diversity of the music scene in the United States. Long before integration between the races became a goal in American society, black and white jazz musicians played together onstage. In the years before women demanded equality, female vocalists such as Ella

Fitzgerald and Billie Holiday were living icons of independent, freethinking women.

Jazz is true American music and represents the creative
musical side of the United States to people across the globe.
Jazz personalities such as Louis Armstrong, Dizzy Gillespie,
Wynton Marsalis, and now Esperanza Spalding, are musical
heroes to countless jazz fans—from Tokyo to Paris to Rio de
Janeiro. Just as a swinging jazz quartet unites its individual
players behind a driving syncopated beat, jazz music has
proven its ability to bring people together through a uni-
versal sound.

*Ella Fitzgerald—
seen here with
Dizzy Gillespie,
right, in 1940—was
an icon of female
independence years
before women
started demanding
equality.*

CHAPTER 1

The Roots of Jazz

At the end of the 1800s, New Orleans, Louisiana, was one of the most exciting cities in the United States. With a population of about two hundred thousand citizens, the city stood at the crossroads of American, French, Spanish, African, and Caribbean cultures. The local music reflected that diversity. Like gumbo, the spicy seafood stew that has long been a favorite of the local citizens, the music of New Orleans was a blend of common and exotic ingredients. The resulting mix was larger than the sum of its parts and formed the foundation of musical innovation for more than 120 years.

New Orleans was originally established by France around 1718. The French citizens who settled in the city had a strong affinity for the arts and music. By the end of the eighteenth century, the city had three opera companies, two symphony orchestras, countless theaters, and several French-language newspapers. New Orleans was so culturally revered that after it became part of the United States in 1803, newspapers referred to the city as "the Paris of America."[4]

The residents of New Orleans were sophisticated, but they also loved to parade and party. Every spring, residents celebrated the Mardi Gras holiday during a carnival season that lasted six to eight weeks. The Mardi Gras festival, based on an ancient Christian tradition, features costumes, parades, and marching bands—a tradition that continues today.

Despite its grand reputation, New Orleans was home to one of the largest slave markets in North America. Tens of thousands of black people who had been kidnapped in West Africa passed through the city on their way to plantations throughout the South. New Orleans was also home to many free blacks who worked as household servants or skilled artisans. These individuals, who made up about 20 percent of the city's population during the early 1800s, created a thriving black subculture.

"A Whirlwind of Musical Activity"

After the end of slavery in 1865, New Orleans became a center of African American culture in the United States. This attracted black people throughout the southern states as well as those living in South America and Caribbean islands such as Haiti, Cuba, and Jamaica. Many of the city's black residents were of mixed African, French, and Spanish ancestry and were known as Creoles. Some light-skinned Creoles identified more closely with European culture than with African or black southern cultures, and those who were musicians were often classically trained. Many Creoles found inspiration not just in the African-based musical traditions of the Caribbean but also in the classical music of Bach, Beethoven, and Mozart.

The multicultural mix in New Orleans was further swelled by sailors from around the world whose ships passed through the city's bustling port—the second busiest in North America. As a major seaport and a popular tourist destination, the streets of New Orleans were lined with bars, brothels, and theaters. The city's freewheeling lifestyle did not sit well with everyone, however, and in 1897 a conservative city alderman named Sidney Story drafted legislation to confine prostitution to one specific neighborhood: an area that soon became known as Storyville.

The owners of the brothels contributed greatly to the development of the city's musical tradition by hiring musicians to entertain their clients. By the beginning of the twentieth century, there were more than 175 places in Storyville where musicians could find work. In addition, New Orleans had hundreds of bars, restaurants, and theaters that catered to the tourist trade. This attracted skilled musicians from across the United States, Europe, and the Caribbean. This cultural gathering yielded an unprecedented mix of musical sounds. As jazz artist and music educator Mark C. Gridley writes:

> New Orleans was a whirlwind of musical activity. Diverse styles were in the air. Opera coexisted with sailor's hornpipes. Music for the European dances of the minuet and quadrille coexisted with African music used in [Haitian] voodoo ceremonies. Band music in the style of . . . [composer] John Philip Sousa [was] quite popular. There were also the work songs of the laborers and the musical cries of street vendors selling their wares.[5]

In this festive atmosphere, it is no wonder New Orleans earned the nickname "The Big Easy," and its motto became *laissez les bons temps roulez* or "let the good times roll."

Spirituals and the Blues

The New Orleans mix of African musical traditions and European styles could be heard in black churches on Sunday. Religious songs called spirituals feature the call-and-response format, which has roots in African tribal music. When singing spirituals, a leader sings a verse and the congregation repeats it in unison. Black musicians in New Orleans composed their own spirituals, adding syncopated swing rhythms and bent-note blues melodies.

The call-and-response style was also found in work songs sung by laborers while picking cotton, hoeing crops, building fences, and laying railroad tracks. Known as field hollers or blues hollers, these songs were heard wherever people labored together in groups.

For more than a century after the US Civil War, southern blacks faced relentless prejudice and poverty. The pain and frustration of their condition found a voice in blues songs that dealt with themes such as loneliness, poverty, home-

The African Roots of Jazz

The ancient tribal music of West Africa has many similarities to jazz. Traditional African music features a strong drumbeat, improvised licks, vocals that imitate instruments, and the use of short, repeated phrases of melody (called "riffs" by jazz musicians). In addition, African roots music is based on a technique known as "call and response," in which a song leader sings a line, and a group of singers repeats that line. Improvised African music was passed orally from generation to generation without written scores.

The drum is central to African music and, like jazz swing, the syncopated rhythm is highly valued. African drummers also use polyrhythm, that is, they create music by using several different rhythms and beats that weave around and intertwine with each other. In addition to drums, traditional African musicians played horns, trumpets, and several types of stringed instruments such as the *banjar*, forerunner to the modern banjo, which was adapted for use in ragtime, jazz, and country music.

lessness, and discrimination. These songs, called twelve-bar blues because they feature twelve measures of music per verse, were incorporated into the music that came to be known as jazz.

Rhythms Move to the Forefront

While blues was an important ingredient in the jazz gumbo, ragtime music was a major component of the emerging style. The word *ragtime* is derived from the concept of ragged time, a technique employed by musicians who used syncopation to give songs a driving momentum.

Ragtime emerged in the mid-1800s when European marches, polkas, and classical works were recast by African Americans. In European music, the succession of musical notes—the melody or tune—is the most important element.

The rhythm plays a secondary role and follows the melody. When the songs were played by African American ragtime musicians, the rhythms became the most important component. This created a ragged sound; complex melodies originally composed without much thought to the rhythm were bent to fit with the driving, syncopated beat. Berendt and Huesmann comment on this mix: "In ragtime, European music and African music met as equals for the first time in America."[6]

Ragtime music was played by brass bands and on banjos and other stringed instruments, but it is most closely associated with the piano. When pianists played ragtime, they used the right hand to "tickle" a melody on the keys. The left hand was used to play an intricate rhythmic bass part.

Scott Joplin wrote the most famous ragtime piece, "Maple Leaf Rag," in 1899.

The most famous ragtime piece, "Maple Leaf Rag," was written by Texas-born composer Scott Joplin in 1899. The song was composed before the era of recorded music, but "Maple Leaf Rag" sold half a million copies in the form of sheet music in a few short years. The popularity of Joplin's composition started a national ragtime fad. By the 1920s, nearly every bar and brothel in the United States featured ragtime ensembles composed of singers, trumpet players, banjo players, drummers, and pianists. During this era, before the term jazz came into common use, most jazz players considered themselves ragtime musicians.

European Influence

Brass and marching bands of European origin made up the final in-

Brass Bands

Michael White, clarinetist and leader of the Original Liberty Jazz Band, describes the sights and sounds of brass band parades in New Orleans:

Boom! . . . Boom! . . . Boom! Those first thunderous blasts from the big bass drum signal the start of a musically led passage deep into the soul of New Orleans.... One, two, even three ten-piece brass bands—each member wearing a uniform and band cap—may line up for the procession. Each group might have three trumpets to improvise melodies, two trombones to slide and growl, a clarinet to sing and dance above the ensemble, and two saxophones to lay down powerful riffs. The foundation is a swinging rhythm section with a lightly rapping snare drum, a roaring bass drum to pour out endless syncopated rhythms, and a whopping tuba to anchor everything with bass lines. Whether jazzing up a standard religious hymn, a traditional march, a popular song, a rag, or a blues, the band struts along and marks the time in easy, neither-too-fast-nor-too-slow dance tempos. . . .

As the parade proceeds, it collects an endless number of "second liners"—hundreds of anonymous onlookers who follow and dance alongside the parade. . . . As the dancing and music reach ever-higher levels of intensity, the participants may feel they're losing themselves in a swirling sea of people, motion, heat, scents, and sounds.

Quoted in John Edward Hasse, ed. *Jazz: The First Century*. New York: William Morrow, 2000, p. 8.

gredient of the New Orleans musical gumbo. Marching bands featured trumpets, trombones, tubas, and drums, and they were extremely popular throughout the United States at the end of the nineteenth century. New Orleans boasted dozens of these ensembles, each with more than twelve members. Musicians in the New Orleans marching bands were almost exclusively black, and they played at events both joyous and sad, such as Mardi Gras celebrations, church dances, and funerals.

In 1909, New Orleans jazz trombonist and blues singer Clyde E.B. Bernhardt was only four years old when he saw his first brass band marching down the street. He remembered the experience clearly seventy-seven years later and described it in his autobiography:

> Suddenly, from around the corner marched these colored men. Oh, they walked so tall and stiff. Bright buttons down the front of their uniforms, red caps on their heads with a round button right in front. As they came closer I saw them playing flashy, shiny instruments that bounced the bright sunshine right in my eyes. Horns all raised up high, blasting so very loud. Some long ones [trombones] sliding in and out. Big fat ones going Umph, Umph. Banjos played fast, drums rat-a-tatting, and a huge round drum that boomed-boomed as it went by.[7]

Musicians in the marching bands often improvised solos to play above the written music. And many of the musicians also played in other bands, performing ragtime, blues, or other styles. As they traveled from one musical setting to the other, they began mixing the many musical styles to form a completely new musical genre.

Buddy Bolden's Blues

No one knows for certain the name of the person who first synthesized ragtime, blues, and marching music into jazz, but the credit is often given to bandleader Charles "Buddy" Bolden, who was born in 1877. Bolden played the cornet, a three-valve brass instrument that resembles a shortened trumpet but has a softer, warmer sound.

Bolden's jazz was based on the rousing spirituals he heard while growing up. As musician and music historian John Edward Hasse writes: "Bolden is said to have been inspired by music of 'holy roller' church, and he delivered sound in many forms, from rough and loud to slow and lowdown."[8] As early as 1901, Bolden was improvising cornet licks with a group composed of a clarinetist, trombonist, guitarist, bassist, and drummer. This musical configuration of players would soon become standard in jazz groups. Bolden played in bars and dance halls throughout greater New Orleans, and he was often seen on Sundays in the city's

Johnson Park playing to large audiences. Although no known recording of Bolden exists, he left behind songs such as "If You Don't Shake, You Don't Get No Cake" and "Funky Butt," which became early jazz standards.

Bolden was a New Orleans legend in his own time. Renowned pianist Jelly Roll Morton describes him: "He drank all the whiskey he could find, never wore a collar and tie, had his shirt busted open so all the girls [could] see that red flannel undershirt, always having a ball—Buddy Bolden was the most powerful [cornet player] in history."[9]

Bolden's behavior was as wild as his music. After being arrested several times for assault, he was declared legally insane in 1907. Bolden was only twenty-nine years old when he was confined to the Louisiana State Asylum where schizophrenia overtook him. He died virtually unknown and unremembered in 1931.

Despite his short lifetime, Bolden's contribution to jazz is unquestioned. British jazz critic Alyn Shipton lists Bolden's musical accomplishments:

Buddy Bolden (second from left) and his band are credited with creating the jazz sound.

Jelly Roll Morton (at piano) with His Red Hot Peppers, including Kid Ory on trombone, in Chicago, Illinois, in 1926.

[Famous] for his sheer volume, Bolden played largely by ear and was credited by many of those who heard him as being the first to bring the explicitly African qualities of flattened blue notes, vocalized tones, and "hot" syncopation into the ragtime setting—in other words, he was seen as the progenitor of improvisation in jazz.[10]

Several New Orleans horn players expanded on the innovations established by Buddy Bolden. The first was Joe Oliver, who assumed the title "Cornet King" in 1907. Oliver was the first player to use rubber cups, derby hats, and other objects known as mutes to cover the bell of his horn. This innovation allowed King Oliver, and later millions of other horn players, to create special effects such as the wah-wah that imitated, in an exaggerated way, the sound of the human voice.

Jelly Roll Morton

Though Bolden is credited for originating the jazz sound, this did not stop the relentless self-promoter Jelly Roll Morton from later claiming, "I invented jazz in 1902."[11] Back in the days when the terms ragtime and jazz were synonymous, Morton even handed out business cards describing himself as "The Creator of Ragtime."[12] While both

claims are exaggerated, there is little doubt that Morton was the first pianist to use improvisation while performing ragtime. He was also the first to highlight the personality of the performer, making his outsized ego as important as the music.

Jelly Roll Morton, born Ferdinand Joseph LaMothe in 1885, was the offspring of light-skinned Creoles in New Orleans. As a young man, Morton worked nightly in the Storyville brothels and earned huge tips for his innovative playing. He used some of the money to have a diamond inserted in his front tooth.

By the 1910s, Morton had transformed the structured sound of ragtime piano into free-flowing jazz creations. He improvised riffs, embellished melodies with cascades of notes, and pounded out a swinging bass rhythm with his left hand. Morton was the first person to write down his jazz improvisations on sheet music. This allowed other musicians across the globe to learn real jazz firsthand from the notes Morton wrote on the page.

Morton began making records in 1923, and he was difficult and exacting in the studio. During recording sessions, he stomped his foot hard to keep the band on time. Drummer Warren "Baby" Dodds recalled that the pounding was so loud it sounded like two bass drums. This interfered with the recording process, so engineers cut a small piece of mattress and put it under Morton's foot to dull the sound. Band members who could not play up to Morton's standards also had problems. Renowned trombonist Edward "Kid" Ory tells a story:

> Zue Robertson was on trombone, and he refused to play the melody of one of the tunes the way Morton wanted it played. Jelly took a big pistol out of his pocket and put it on the piano, and Robertson played the melody note for note.[13]

Taking Jazz on the Road

Other musicians saw to it that jazz spread beyond its original base in New Orleans. Kid Ory moved to Los Angeles, California, in 1914, making him the first person to take jazz music to the West. Kid Ory's Original Creole Band was famous for its loud, ragged style, known as tailgate. The Original Creole Band toured the United States continually, playing for white audiences in vaudeville theaters and introducing audiences to the New Orleans sound. In 1922, Ory and his band became the first African Americans from New Orleans to record jazz music.

Cornet player Freddie Keppard played with Ory, and his creative sounds helped make the Original Creole Band very popular. As pianist Jelly Roll Morton said, "There was no end to his ideas. . . . He could play a chorus eight or ten different ways."[14] One story often repeated about Keppard says that he was offered the chance to make the first jazz record by the Victor Talking Machine Company, but he turned Victor down because he was afraid that someone would hear the record and steal his licks.

Sidney Bechet's Genius

While Keppard and Ory introduced jazz to a wider audience in the United States, Sidney Bechet played a central role in developing the clarinet as a solo instrument in jazz. During his long career, he brought jazz music to the attention of the world.

Born in 1897, Bechet learned to play the clarinet as a little boy. He got to play with adults for the first time in 1907 at his brother's birthday party when Freddie Keppard's band was hired to provide music. The band's clarinetist, George Baquet, was late for the gig, so the ten-year-old Bechet picked up his clarinet and jammed along with the band. He was so good that when Baquet finally arrived, the two clarinetists played side-by-side all night long.

By the time Bechet was thirteen, he worked with some of the most renowned brass bands in New Orleans. In 1917 he hit the road, touring the United States playing the soprano saxophone (an instrument modeled on the clarinet but made of brass). In 1919 Bechet became one of the first jazz players to tour Europe, and his music was praised by the highly respected Swiss conductor Ernest Ansermet, who said Bechet was "an extraordinary clarinet virtuoso . . . and

Sidney Bechet records "Summertime" in 1939. He was key in the establishment of the clarinet as a solo instrument in jazz.

artist of genius [who played jazz songs] equally admirable for their richness of invention, force of accent, and daring in novelty and the unexpected."[15]

Jazz Goes on Record

By the mid-1910s, jazz musicians from New Orleans were traveling across the United States playing for large, appreciative audiences. These acts were largely Creole and African American, but it was not long before white bands got into the act. The Original Dixieland Jazz Band (ODJB), led by Italian American cornetist Nick La Rocca, profited from the popularity of this new musical trend. Curiously, this New Orleans–based Dixieland group had never heard the term jazz until they played in Chicago, Illinois, in 1916. As La Rocca told an interviewer, "We only called the music 'jazz' after someone in the audience one night in Chicago kept hollering at us to "Jazz it up!", and it seemed to fit our music. No, I never heard the word in New Orleans. I found out later it was a [curse] word in Chicago, but I guess we purified it."[16]

The ODJB moved on to New York City in 1917, landing a gig at the prestigious Reisenweber's restaurant. At first the crowds were hostile toward the musicians because they were unable to understand their swinging, ragtime sound. Within a few weeks, however, people began to appreciate the music for its syncopated, danceable beat. The ODJB became a sensation, drawing huge crowds that lined up around the block waiting to get in to Reisenweber's. The band went on to perform at the club for eighteen months.

Spotting a profitable trend, Victor Record executives ushered the group into the recording studio, and the ODJB became the first jazz band to make a record. When "Livery Stable Blues" was released in March 1917, it sold 250,000 copies within months. At that time no other record—classical, opera, marching band, or any other style—had ever sold

The Original Dixieland Jazz Band was the first jazz band to make a record, in March of 1917.

The Jazz Drum Set

Jazz has always been rhythm based, and early drummers assembled a wide variety of drums into a "kit." These improvised drum sets have become standard equipment for drummers playing any type of music. The main jazz beat was laid down on a snare, a small drum with a strand of wire stretched across the bottom head. When struck on top, the snare gives a sustained rattle, or "sizzle" sound. A basic kit was rounded out with several small bass drums called tom-toms and a few cymbals. Anything that could enhance the rhythm, such as a cowbell, anvil, and woodblock, was added.

Another addition to the drum kit was invented by jazz drummer Warren "Baby" Dodds around 1920. Dodds added a foot-operated pedal to thump on his big bass drum. Around that time, a Turkish cymbal maker Zildjian, who had been in business for almost five hundred years, began selling high-quality cymbals throughout the United States. Zildjian provided drummers with crash and sizzle cymbals—named for their tone—and ride cymbals, which are continually tapped, or ridden. Finally, innovative drummer Vic Berton added two small cymbals, about thirteen inches across, to a pedal-operated stand, or "high hat," and the modern drum kit was complete.

such an astonishing number. "Livery Stable Blues" would eventually sell millions of copies throughout the world.

Some critics found the music of the ODJB extremely comical: They played fast and furious with the drummer pounding out a heavy beat while the cornet and clarinet improvised on the high notes and the saxophones and trombone looped through running bass and melody lines. The sound turned ragtime jazz into a musical version of the slapstick comedy seen in popular movies by Charlie Chaplin and Buster Keaton. The hilarity was heightened at a break in the "Livery Stable Blues" where the cornet imitates the sound of a horse whinny, the clarinet in response sounds like a crowing rooster, and the trombone rips out the sound of a braying donkey.

Although the public snapped up the records of the ODJB, critics panned the music, calling it crude and harsh. The music also found critics within the African American jazz community. Many felt that the white version of jazz was "cleaned up" and less authentic than the music invented by black musicians.

A New Era in Music

By 1919, the efforts of Bolden, Oliver, Ory, and the ODJB ushered in a new music era. The jazz musicians differentiated their new art form from ragtime, blues, and marching music in several important ways: The melodies were improvised and when five or seven players jammed together, the sound was far wilder and more complex than ragtime. In addition, jazz band leaders wrote much of their own music instead of following scores by professional composers.

By 1920, jazz music was heard live in Los Angeles, Chicago, New York, London, and Paris as well as in New Orleans. Jazz records were selling across the globe. The music that was once confined to the sordid brothels of the Big Easy found new respectability in theaters and concert halls. At the dawn of the Roaring Twenties, jazz music was poised to take the world by storm.

CHAPTER 2

Swingin' Jazz Bands

The 1920s were known as the Roaring Twenties and the Jazz Age. It was one of the most unique decades in US history. The US economy was growing at its fastest rate ever, the stock market soared, and a new class of millionaires was minted virtually overnight. The first radios were mass-produced in 1920 and within a few years, nearly every home in the United States owned one. The popularity of records was also growing because of advances in recording technology and record production.

Radio and records helped make jazz immensely popular in northern cities such as New York, New York, and Chicago, Illinois, where there was an increasing demand for jazz acts. This prompted a mass exodus of African American jazz musicians from New Orleans, Louisiana. Many were booked in fancy clubs catering to white patrons. This unprecedented meeting of the races had jazz music at its center. As black music critic J.A. Rogers wrote in *Survey* magazine in 1925, "Jazz has come to stay because it is an expression of the times, of the breathless, energetic, superactive times in which we are living. . . . The [African American] musicians of America are playing a great part in this change. . . . They are not hampered by conventions or traditions, and with their new ideas, their constant experiment, they are causing new blood to flow in the veins of music."[17]

Armstrong Comes to Town

In the 1920s, Chicago was at the center of the Jazz Age. The city's clubs featured all-star bands, such as King Oliver's Creole Jazz Band and the New Orleans Rhythm Kings. With so many musicians flooding into one town, only the best performers were able to rise above the crowd. The top instrumentalists were able to differentiate themselves by playing the most unusual solos and the fastest riffs. As a result, the 1920s emerged as the era of the solo player, led by one of the greatest musicians in jazz history, cornetist Louis Armstrong.

Armstrong arrived in Chicago on August 8, 1922. He stepped off the train with only his battered horn and a

Louis Armstrong's ability to hit high notes out of reach of other trumpeters established him as one of the greatest jazz musicians in history.

threadbare tuxedo to perform in. Although he was poor, Armstrong had something money could not buy: a phenomenal tone, a gift for improvisation, and the ability to blow his horn in an upper register out of the reach of other trumpeters. Armstrong was invited to the Windy City by King Oliver, who had been nurturing the young musician for years in New Orleans.

Armstrong was born in 1901 in a neighborhood so rough that it was known as "The Battlefield." Arrested at the age of eleven for firing a gun into the air on New Year's Eve, Armstrong was placed in a juvenile detention center called the Colored Waif's Home. He picked up a battered trumpet for five dollars and was quickly acknowledged as the best horn player in the home's marching band. The first time Armstrong led the band as it paraded through Storyville, listeners on balconies and sidewalks rewarded their incredible sound with such generous tips that the school had enough money to buy all new instruments for the band.

After he was released in 1913, Armstrong began playing the toughest brothels in Storyville, where his loud, clear improvisations became legend. Because his cheeks puffed out so far when he blew his horn, he was given many nicknames, including Gate-mouth, Rhythm Jaws, Dippermouth, and Satchelmouth. The last name, abbreviated to Satchmo, stuck, and Armstrong would be referred to by that moniker for the rest of his life.

After arriving in Chicago, Armstrong spent two years playing with Oliver's Creole Jazz Band. The group featured Johnny Dodds on clarinet, his brother "Baby" Dodds on drums, Honoré Dutrey on trombone, Bill Johnson on banjo and bass, and Lil Hardin on piano. The Creole Jazz Band filled a nightclub called Lincoln Gardens with black jazz fans every week. Satchmo had the uncanny ability to complement Oliver's improvisations so closely that their music sounded as though they were playing from written scores. Whatever riff or line Oliver would invent, Armstrong could play in harmony a quarter beat behind. People cheered as Oliver and Armstrong traded cornet solos, played riffs in unison, and created the most danceable beat on the street. As word spread about Armstrong's talents, white people began coming to the club as well, eager to hear the New Orleans phenomenon.

In April 1923, the Creole Jazz Band cut its first records in the studio. The song "Dippermouth Blues" jumped off the shelves in record stores as well as "Jazzin' Babies' Blues," "Snake Rag," and other songs featuring Oliver and Armstrong's dueling cornets.

Armstrong married Lil Hardin in 1924. She was a talented musician in her own right: a pianist, singer, composer, and arranger. His ambitious wife encouraged Armstrong to leave Oliver's band. He headed for the big time in New York City, playing a thirteen-month stint with the Fletcher Henderson Orchestra. After the New York engagements, Armstrong moved back to Chicago to play with Lil's band at the Dreamland Café. During this period, Satchmo began singing and belting out songs in the raspy vocal style that became his trademark.

Musical Firsts

Between November 1925 and December 1928, Armstrong formed several bands, known as the Hot Five and the Hot Seven. These groups of five or seven all-star players only performed for recording sessions, and their music became some of the most influential in jazz history. Armstrong took extended solos and allowed the other musicians the same courtesy. This permanently elevated the role of the virtuoso solo performer. On "Gut Bucket Blues," Armstrong even introduces players by name as they take solos, a first in recording history.

Another jazz first, for which Armstrong deserves credit, was the result of a happy accident. During the 1926 recording of "Heebie Jeebies," Armstrong accidentally dropped his lyric sheet on the floor. Rather than stop the music, the record producer motioned for Satchmo to make up some words. Armstrong improvised a string of nonsensical syllables with vocal growls and rumbles meant to sound like a deeply soulful trumpet solo. This was the first recording of the technique known as scat singing. When "Heebie Jeebies" was released, scat became one of the hottest styles among jazz singers.

The Hot Band records highlight Satchmo at the height of his creative peak. Shipton describes their importance:

> [The discs] confirmed that Armstrong had successfully combined emotional depth, rhythmic innovation, and a liberating sense of solo freedom into a heady and original mixture. He pushed at the boundaries of the cornet's range. . . . Overall, he brought a new set of [creative] qualities into jazz, a sense that there could be considerable artistic worth in music conceived as popular entertainment.[18]

Developing the Chicago Sound

When not recording, Armstrong played to mostly black audiences on Chicago's South Side. But as early as 1923, when Satchmo was still playing with King Oliver, a group of teenage white boys began sneaking into his performances. These young men were from an upper-class West Side Chicago neighborhood known as Austin and attended Austin High School.

Members of what became known as the Austin High Gang included clarinetists Benny Goodman and Pee Wee Russell, horn player and singer Jack Teagarden, drummer David Tough, saxophone player Bud Freeman, and guitarist Eddie Condon. The group of boys, many of whom were in the school band, first heard jazz on records in a neighborhood ice cream parlor. After wearing out the grooves on several records, the boys—some still too young to drive—rode their bicycles down to the South Side to hear live jazz.

At first, the patrons of the club were hostile to the white schoolboys. But Oliver, who always believed in helping young musicians, nodded to them from the stage. The crowd eventually accepted the young outsiders into their midst. In *Jazz: A Film by Ken Burns*, trumpeter Wynton Marsalis explains the fascination of the young musicians:

> [When] these white kids come . . . to hear King Oliver and Louis Armstrong playing this music, we have to realize that this is some of the most abstract and sophisticated music that anybody has ever heard, short

of Bach. And . . . they're attracted to the groove and the feeling of the music . . . and they're saying, "Man, this is what we want to play like."[19]

After graduating from high school, the Austin High Gang began playing engagements around Chicago with their own style. They blended New Orleans jazz and an aggressive, northern beat more reminiscent of the rat-tat-tat of a machine gun. This sound was distinctive and soon became known as the Chicago style.

Ella Fitzgerald Sings and Swings

Ella Fitzgerald, known as the "First Lady of Song," seemed an unlikely candidate for jazz stardom. In 1934, she was living in poverty on the streets of New York. On a dare, she entered an amateur talent contest at Harlem's Apollo Theater and won the twenty-five-dollar prize money. Fitzgerald was soon introduced to drummer Chick Webb, who reluctantly agreed to hire the inexperienced singer for a single night. The crowd loved Fitzgerald's beautiful voice, and Webb kept her on for a weeklong engagement at the Savoy. Before long, Fitzgerald developed unmatched improvisation and scat abilities and began making records with the Chick Webb Orchestra.

In 1938, Fitzgerald converted the nursery rhyme "A-tisket, A-tasket" into a huge hit record for Webb. This was followed up by the song "Undecided." When Webb unexpectedly died in 1939, his band was renamed "Ella Fitzgerald and Her Famous Orchestra." Fitzgerald took on the role of bandleader and recorded nearly 150 sides with the orchestra before it broke up in 1942. When the big-band era ended in the 1950s, Fitzgerald went on to become an international pop star recording songs by composers Cole Porter, Duke Ellington, Richard Rodgers, and Lorenz Hart.

Duke Ellington's Toodle-Oo

Duke Ellington (at piano) jams with other jazz musicians, including Dizzy Gillespie (foreground), in 1943.

Although Chicago remained an important center for jazz during the 1920s, New York City—a town jazz musicians had named "the Big Apple"—was a worthy rival. By 1920, New York had more African American residents than any other US city. Most African Americans lived in the vibrant Harlem neighborhood. Harlem was at the center of a growing creative movement among black poets, painters, musicians, and authors known as the Harlem Renaissance. Jazz was the sound of the Harlem Renaissance and the music could be heard in the neighborhood blasting out of record players, radios, and bar rooms night and day.

Edward "Duke" Ellington was a young pianist born in 1899 in Washington, D.C. Ellington was the king of New York jazz. He moved to Harlem in 1923, and by the

mid-1920s he had formed his own red-hot band, The Washingtonians. The group combined the ragtime jazz piano Ellington recalled from his youth with Armstrong's improvisational style.

Trumpet player Bubber Miley gave The Washingtonians a unique voice when he used his mute to obtain a down-and-dirty, blues-drenched, "gut bucket" effect. Ellington called it the jungle sound. The recording of "East St. Louis Toodle-Oo" is a good example of this jazz strain. Describing it, Ellington said that Miley was "the body and soul of Soulville. He was raised on soul and saturated and marinated in soul. Every note he played was soul."[20]

By 1927, Ellington began mixing jazz with the lush orchestral sounds heard in popular music and theatrical musicals. By using strings, brass, and woodwinds, Ellington forged a sound all his own. Critics responded positively and began to describe Ellington's music as sophisticated.

Ellington's big break came in 1927 when his group became the house band for the Cotton Club. Although it was located in Harlem and all the waitstaff and entertainers were black, the expensive nightclub catered only to white people. The ten-piece band, now renamed Duke Ellington and His Cotton Club Orchestra, quickly achieved national fame when its performances were featured in radio broadcasts. With his newfound fame and money, Ellington was able to hire the best musicians in New York, and he wrote stunning arrangements that allowed them to showcase their talents.

Between 1927 and 1931, Ellington and his orchestra made 150 records in sixty-four different recording sessions. Ellington's many memorable compositions, such as "Mood Indigo," "Sophisticated Lady," and "Take the 'A' Train" utilized catchy and unusual melodies that bridged the gap between 1920s jazz combos and the big-band era of the 1930s. Today Ellington's sophisticated sounds are considered jazz classics across the globe.

Big-Band Jazz

The Jazz Age came to a crashing halt in October 1929 when the stock market crashed, ushering in the Great Depression.

Despite tough economic times, people continued to go out and dance to jazz music. During a time when unemployment hovered at 33 percent and large families were crammed into tiny apartments, dance halls offered young people an escape from the harsh realities of daily life. For seventy-five cents, couples could swing the night away to big-band music at dance halls found in cities large and small.

Big-band swing melded the styles of Armstrong and Ellington. The sound was inspired by Satchmo's swinging jazz rhythms mixed with Ellington's sophisticated sound. Big-band jazz featured the most talented musicians, playing tight, fast, and with great agility. Big bands incorporated twelve to twenty musicians and utilized instruments not previously heard in jazz, including saxophones, cymbals, and guitars. The New Orleans–style ragtime banjos were swapped for guitars and the marching band tubas were traded for string basses. Music critic Gary Giddins describes how big-band instruments were arranged:

> Basically you have four sections in a big band. You've got the saxophone section [and] the reed section, which often has clarinets. You have the trumpet section and the trombone section which became more important as the years went by. . . . And then you have the rhythm section which was . . . just drums, bass and piano. And these sections work like gears in a machine. They interlock and what the [arranger] has to do is to find really exciting, inventive ways to blend these instruments, to work one section against another and to create a new music.[21]

Because of the large size of swing bands, musicians could not readily improvise as they might have playing with Armstrong. The overall big-band sound relied on composed arrangements, while improvisation was limited to soloists. Larger orchestras also needed conductors to stand center stage waving batons to unify performers, set the tempo, and keep the beat. With conductors, composers, and soloists playing a greater role in swing bands, several bandleaders who excelled at these tasks became nationally famous. Trombonist Glenn Miller, clarinetist Benny Goodman, pianist William "Count" Basie, and saxophonists Coleman Hawkins and

Billie Holiday Is Lady Day

No vocalist is more associated with the swing era than Billie Holiday, also known as Lady Day. Born into poverty in 1915, Holiday perfected her singing while working in a brothel in 1929. During the 1930s, she sang in jazz clubs in Harlem. Holiday was discovered by producer and talent scout John Hammond who arranged a recording session with Benny Goodman in 1935. In the years that followed, Holiday recorded with dozens of jazz superstars including Lester Young, Count Basie, and Louis Armstrong. When she sang with Artie Shaw in 1938, Holiday was one of the first black singers ever featured in concert with a white orchestra.

Holiday forever changed jazz singing by adopting Armstrong's vocal style. Like Satchmo, Holiday tweaked the rhythm for emphasis and rewrote melodies to fit her mood. Although her high voice lacked range, she was able to inject songs with a strong emotional delivery. Audiences were gripped by Holiday's almost girlish singing, which belied her troubled soul. Lady Day's promising career was cut short in the early 1940s

At the height of her career, Billie Holiday performs at Carnegie Hall in New York City in 1948.

by self-destructive behavior, which included alcohol and heroin abuse. Although she died a broken woman in 1959, Holiday's soul-stirring vocal style and classic compositions, including "God Bless the Child" and "Lady Sings the Blues," continue to inspire.

Lester Young produced music that was so distinctive their names have become synonymous with big-band jazz.

Swing bands often featured vocalists who could sing written arrangements or scat improvised melodies. The

The Savoy Ballroom in the Harlem neighborhood of New York City was nicknamed "the Home of Happy Feet."

status of the singer changed, however, over the course of the swing era. During the early 1930s, bands and their conductors were the main attractions at the ballrooms. Singers were referred to as standup vocalists because they would sit in a chair by the side of the stage. They only appeared front and center when it was time to stand up and sing a song or two. That changed in the late 1930s when singers such as Ella Fitzgerald, Sarah Vaughn, Billie Eckstine, Frank Sinatra, and Billie Holiday achieved prominence. By the end of World War II in 1945, these talented vocalists were considered major attractions and took center stage.

Heights of Popularity

Whether the attraction was the singer, the conductor, or the instrumentalists, there was little doubt that big-band swing was the dominant form of popular entertainment. Hasse describes how swing transformed American culture:

> Swing music and dancing became a huge phenomenon, almost a national obsession, taking jazz to heights of popularity never achieved before or since. . . . Never before had jazz so dominated the field of popular music. At no other time was jazz such a catalyst for thousands of fans queuing up for a performance, for turn-away crowds so large and enthusiastic that the police had to be called in to keep order, for so many live radio broadcasts carrying the music to waiting listeners coast-to-coast, and for heated band battles that became the stuff of legends.[22]

Big-band jazz was performed in glittering ballrooms known as dance palaces. Inside the ballrooms, dance crazes rose and fell in popularity throughout the swing era. Dance steps with names such as the lindy hop, the Suzy Q, the shim-sham-shimmy, and the shag swept across the nation. Many of these popular dances were invented by African American patrons at Harlem's Savoy Ballroom, whose nickname was "the Home of Happy Feet."[23]

Fletcher Henderson

Pianist and composer Fletcher Henderson was one of the premier acts featured at the Savoy. Henderson pioneered some of the fundamentals of big-band swing, such as contrasting reed and brass sections against one another and having entire sections perform the call-and-response technique.

Musicians in Henderson's band were expected to read and play music expertly arranged by saxophonist Don Redman. The band served as a proving ground for many soloists who would go on to become stars in their own right, including trumpeter Cootie Williams, trombonists Charlie Green and Benny Morton, tenor saxophonist Chu Berry, and alto sax player Benny Carter.

A National Obsession

Musician and music historian John Edward Hasse describes the social and cultural phenomena created by swing music in the 1930s:

Public dancing became, by the 1930s, one of the key American courtship rituals. For many young people, swing music and dancing served as important emotional outlets; for others, they offered much-needed escape from the economic difficulties of the lingering Depression. With partner in hand, caught up in shared euphoria and momentary forgetfulness, dancers could stomp and swing themselves into states of [tranquility]. . . . Ears flooded with irresistible melodies and intoxicating rhythms, skin flushed with excitement (and perhaps desire), and pulses quickened as [people danced] the nights, and their cares, away. . . . Most of the dancers were young people, and swing took center stage in American youth culture, just as rock and roll would two decades later. . . .

Bands had always competed for popularity, but in the Swing Era competition between dance bands came to the fore, taking on the characteristics of rivalry between great athletic teams. Bands attracted ardent followers, orchestras engaged in sometimes epic band battles, and jazz magazines and black newspapers ran readers' polls to select the top groups. Fans kept track of changes in bands' personnel and argued the merits of one band over another.

John Edward Hasse, ed. *Jazz: The First Century*. New York: William Morrow, 2000, p. 56.

Henderson offered some of his best arrangements, such as "King Porter Stomp," "Sometimes I'm Happy," and "Down South Camp Meeting," to Benny Goodman. Although these were huge hits, Henderson's band was little known outside of New York. Despite his swing innovations, Henderson's band struggled financially, finally breaking up in 1934.

Coleman Hawkins (bottom right) established the saxophone as a serious solo instrument.

Hot and Cool

Tenor sax player Coleman Hawkins was one of the most celebrated musicians to come out of Henderson's band. Hawkins was only eighteen years old when he was hired by Henderson in 1923. At that time, the saxophone was rarely used in jazz. But the improvisational genius of Louis Armstrong on trumpet—and his ability to hit high notes— inspired Hawkins to make the saxophone a brilliant solo instrument, on par with the trumpet or clarinet. According to Giddins, Coleman Hawkins:

> had the most virile sound I've ever heard on a tenor saxophone. It was big and full without being blustery, without a lot of wind or extra vibrato. And he just played with such authority, I mean every eight bars in a solo would just seem to . . . unfurl like a perfect ribbon. [There] was never any hesitation or any question, any unnecessary repetition. Extraordinary eloquence.[24]

Hawkins found a rival in Lester Young, a New Orleans– based sax player who began his career playing in his family's traveling show. Whereas Hawkins's style has been described as "hot," Young pioneered the "cool" jazz sound that was light, flowing, delicate, and used no throbbing vibrato.

Young gained national recognition after joining pianist Count Basie's band in 1934. His 1936 recordings with Basie influenced countless other saxophone players, many of whom imitated Young's solos note for note.

The Kansas City Stomp

Young initially jammed with Basie in Kansas City, Missouri, where the growing jazz scene rivaled that of Chicago or New York. Located in the geographical center of the United States, Kansas City attracted hundreds of swing musicians from coast to coast. These musicians brought their own regional styles along with them. Like New Orleans in the early 1900s, Kansas City became a melting pot of jazz styles. The musicians blended blues and swing with boogie-woogie, a style known for its fast tempo and kicking rhythm. They added "shout" vocals in which singers boisterously yelled out lyrics. The new style was easy to dance to and appropriately called stomp or jump blues.

As might be expected, competition was fierce, and Kansas City musicians were expected to excel at all styles. As jazz pianist Jay McShann remembers:

> [If] you didn't swing in Kansas City, you hadn't said nothing. Then if you couldn't play . . . pretty, sweet music, like "Stardust" and stuff like that, you hadn't said anything. Then if you couldn't play boogie-woogie, you hadn't said anything. And if you couldn't play the blues, you hadn't said anything. See, in Kansas City you didn't just do one thing—you had to do the whole bit.[25]

Jumpin' with Basie

With his rapid-fire piano pounding, Count Basie was the greatest of the stomp jazz musicians. His compositions such as "One O'Clock Jump" and "Jumpin' at the Woodside" display a foot-stomping, finger-snapping beat that propels the horn solos forward with a rhythmic power. The music burns with an intensity rarely heard in big-band swing.

Basie's eight-piece band played a regular gig at the Reno Club in Kansas City throughout 1936, and the shows were broadcast nationally over KXBY radio every night. The music caught the ear of New York producer John Hammond, who persuaded Basie to come to New York in early 1937. Within a year, Basie burst onto the national scene with several songs hitting the top of the music charts.

The King of Swing

Basie's music was red-hot, dynamic and imaginative, but the acknowledged king of swing during the mid-1930s was Benny Goodman. Although Goodman's style was not as adventurous and exciting as Basie's, his smooth, polished sound appealed to a larger audience.

Goodman has been given credit for kicking off the national swing craze in 1934 when he put together his first twelve-piece band using Henderson as his arranger. Goodman wanted to perfect a sound that would reach out

Benny Goodman, center on clarinet, and his band play in Newark, New Jersey, in 1937 during the swing craze.

to young people who filled dance halls and purchased a majority of jazz records. To attract this group, Goodman believed a swing band still needed to have a small-combo sound. He later recalled, "I was interested only in jazz. I wanted to create a tight, small-band quality, and I wanted every one of my boys to be a soloist. The band had to have a driving beat, a rhythmic brass section, and a sax section that would be smooth with lots of punch."[26] Goodman achieved the sound he was hoping for, hiring players such as Bunny Berigan on trumpet, Jess Stacey on piano, Helen Ward on vocals, and revolutionary beat wizard Gene Krupa on drums.

Goodman's popularity exploded when he played the Palomar Ballroom in Los Angeles on August 21, 1935. When Goodman broke into his trademark sound, the students in the sold-out audience went wild, nearly causing a riot. After this engagement, Goodman traveled back to New York, where massive crowd commotion ensued when his band played. From that point on, Goodman was gold. He scored dozens of top-ten hits including "Moonglow," "Body and Soul," and "Bugle Call Rag," and played the prestigious Carnegie Hall at a time when swing had never been heard in a concert-hall setting. Band members such as Krupa and trumpeter Harry James became so famous that they started their own bands to capitalize on the swing craze.

One of the lasting effects of Goodman's popularity was the breakdown of racial barriers. The Jewish clarinetist openly admired African American jazz musicians and put together one of the first racially mixed bands in 1935. The group featured African American Teddy Wilson on piano, Lionel Hampton on vibes, and string virtuoso Charlie Christian on electric guitar.

Goodman also broke down gender barriers when he

Glenn Miller

Unlike most of his big city, big-band colleagues, trombonist, composer, and arranger Glenn Miller was born on a farm in Iowa. He lived in rural areas until he moved to New York City in 1928. Miller was a driven, ambitious perfectionist who disdained wild improvisation and insisted band members play his well-crafted arrangements in a precise, smooth manner. Glenn Miller and His Orchestra made dozens of records between 1939 and 1942 and was one of the most popular big bands in the country. The orchestra's classic hits include "Tuxedo Junction," "Chattanooga Choo Choo," "Moonlight Serenade," and "In the Mood."

When the United States entered World War II in 1941, Miller walked away from his $20,000-a-week salary and enlisted in the army. On December 15, 1944, Miller was flying from London to Paris in a small plane. He was on his way to perform concerts in hospitals for US troops and those on leave from recent heavy fighting. Miller's plane went down somewhere over the English Channel, and his remains were never found. His official status remains missing in action to this day.

hired singer Helen Ward at a time when few swing bands had female vocalists. Goodman correctly assumed that Ward's presence would attract male college students to his gigs. With the stunning success of Goodman's band, others began hiring female singers.

The End of the Big Band

Despite the popularity of performers like Benny Goodman, big-band jazz was hit hard when the United States entered World War II in 1941. Musicians were drafted into the military, and there was a shortage of basic goods needed for touring such as gasoline, tires, and the brass and silver used to make musical instruments. The swing bands that remained intact joined in the war effort, playing concerts for US troops throughout North America and Europe. Some jazz entertainers gave more than their time and talents. One of the greatest big-band leaders, Glenn Miller, died on his way to a show when his plane went down over the English Channel on December 15, 1944.

The end of the war in 1945 brought no recovery for the big-band business. The wild teenagers who lindy hopped their blues away during the Great Depression had grown up. When millions of soldiers returned home, dancing and swinging gave way to buying homes, raising babies, and going to work. In December 1946, eight top bandleaders—Woody Herman, Benny Goodman, Harry James, Les Brown, Jack Teagarden, Benny Carter, Ina Ray Hutton, and Tommy Dorsey—announced they were quitting the business. The sounds of big-band swing that had once rung through the streets and alleys of cities large and small faded to silence.

CHAPTER 3

The Birth of Bebop

After World War II ended in 1945, big-band swing was deemed passé, or out of fashion, by the record buying public. To many in the prosperous postwar period, the swinging sound of the Depression years seemed irrelevant. As many Americans married, settled down, and had children, they began to listen to romantic ballads that featured smooth-voiced crooners such as Frank Sinatra, who sang catchy melodies backed by lush string orchestras. Even innovative jazz singers such as Ella Fitzgerald and Sarah Vaughn began to record mainstream pop music so that they could survive in the rapidly changing music business.

New Sounds, New Scales

Even as the commercial demand for big-band music evaporated, black jazz instrumentalists continued to gather in smoky bar rooms in New York City to jam. Liberated from earlier constraints of having to please mainstream audiences, musicians at these sessions broke the traditional rules of swing. They introduced new concepts to create a style of jazz that came to be known as bop or bebop.

The term for the style is taken from a Dizzy Gillespie tune, "Bebop," recorded in 1945. The sound differed from big-band swing in many significant ways: Bebop was played by small combos, as opposed to large bands. The tempo of bebop was fast—in its most frenzied form almost twice as fast as the average swing dance tune. Bebop rarely featured the clarinet, made famous by Benny Goodman. Instead the music was driven by the trumpet, saxophone, standup bass, drums, and piano. Drums were especially important to the beat of bebop. Instead of providing a steady background beat, drummers provided polyrhythms that interacted with the horns.

Bebop musicians valued innovation, improvisation, and hot licks above all else. To play bebop, a musician had to be extremely proficient on his instrument, because the melodies, harmonies, and rhythms of the music were much more complex. In addition, the music was based solely on improvisation—there were few written musical arrangements, and if there was a score it was used more as a rough outline rather than as a detailed blueprint for the musicians.

In technical terms, bebop utilized a different musical scale than previously found in Western music. Earlier jazz melodies and harmonies were based on the traditional seven-note or diatonic scale. This scale was often memorized by schoolchildren who sang "do-re-mi-fa-so-la-ti." Bebop is played using chromatic scales. Chromatic scales are made up of twelve notes of the scale including the semitones—the sharp and flat notes—between the seven notes of the diatonic scale. Although some listeners think bebop jazz music sounds discordant, the chromatic scale provides a greatly increased range for the jazz soloist.

While bebop was a delight to sophisticated listeners, it was most definitely *not* dance music. Its speedy tempos and shifting beats frightened away many dancers. And while sax and trumpet players may have been excited by the cascading and surprising licks, it was not music the average listener found relaxing. In the mainstream press, bebop was described as overheated, racing, nervous, and fragmented. The sounds also irritated old-school jazz musicians. Benny Goodman claimed bebop players were "not real musicians," while Louis Armstrong condemned "all them weird chords which don't mean nothing . . . you got no melody to remember and no beat to dance to."[27] Beboppers responded by referring to the older generation of jazz players as "moldy figs."[28]

Jamming at Minton's

The birth of bebop is attributed to several jazz giants: Dizzy Gillespie, saxophonist Charlie Parker, pianist Thelonious Monk, and drummer Kenny Clarke. These men were influenced by an earlier generation of innovative swing players such as saxophonists Lester Young and Coleman Hawkins, pianist Art Tatum, guitarist Charlie Christian, and bassist Jimmy Blanton.

The pioneers of bebop began their careers in swing bands led by Cab Calloway, Earl Hines, and Billy Eckstine. During this period, the bebop innovators performed swing for white audiences early in the evening and then traveled to Harlem nightclubs for afterhours jams. Because most players did not have the freedom to let their creative juices flow during their regular performances, Harlem jams often turned into cutting sessions where players attempted to out-play each other with nearly impossible riffs and experimentation runs.

Monday night bebop jams, when few jazz musicians had gigs, were particularly productive. In the late 1940s, in order to attract a crowd on the slowest night of the week, the manager of a Harlem club called Minton's offered free food and drink to musicians who would come in and play. Before long, these open stage jams began to attract the hippest crowds in New York.

The house band at Minton's consisted of Clarke, Monk, bassist Nick Fenton, and trumpet player Joe Guy. They were often joined by Gillespie and Parker. As word of these jam sessions spread, New York's finest players made the pilgrimage to Minton's on Monday nights. As might be expected, the competition was brutal. Musicians who were not of the first rank were often blown off the stage by the house band's players who would randomly change keys, play difficult rhythms, and use other tricks to separate the truly talented from the hopeful amateurs. The players

Jazz on the Street

New York's 52nd Street was once lined with so many jazz clubs it was known simply as "The Street" by musicians and fans alike. This center of the postwar jazz universe is described by music journalist Tad Lathrop:

It was called "Swing Street" and "the street that never slept." In its nightclub heyday—which lasted roughly from 1933 to the late forties—the stretch of Manhattan's 52nd Street that ran between Fifth and Seventh Avenues served as a vibrant center of jazz activity.

Clubs such as the Onyx, the Famous Door, and the Three Deuces

Fifty-second Street in New York City was known as "Swing Street" during its heyday in the 1930s and 1940s.

lit the street in neon. Over time, they also cast light on the changing face of jazz. In the late thirties, a walk past a club marquee and downstairs into a basement would plunge a visitor into a crowded, smoke-filled setting alive with the sounds of swing. Ten years later, that same descent would emerge the clubgoer in the hyperkinetic energy of bebop. . . .

It was on the Street that many heard sax innovator Charlie Parker for the first time, when he would drop in unannounced to jam. "Everybody just flipped," clarinetist Tony Scott recalls. Parker's influence would course through the Street's echoing basements and into future jazz.

Quoted in John Edward Hasse, ed. *Jazz: The First Century.* New York: William Morrow, 2000, p. 94.

would also challenge out-of-towners, as pianist Hampton Hawes recalls:

> One night at Minton's . . . somebody recognized me and said, "There's a cat from California supposed to play good, let's get him up here." Now at that time there were a lot of East Coast musicians who thought it slick to try to shoot down anyone new on the scene who was starting to make a reputation. It was like an initiation, a ceremonial rite . . . calling far-out tunes in strange keys with the hip changes at tempos so fast if you didn't fly you fell—that's how you earned your diploma in the University of the Streets of New York.
>
> For a week I had watched these cats burning each other up, ambushing outsiders, [messing] up their minds so bad they would fold and split the stand after one tune. Surprised by their coldness because they were so friendly off the stand, I [guessed] that I wasn't quite ready. . . . No point in selling tickets if you don't have a show.[29]

"Klook-Mop" Clarke Rides a New Rhythm

One musical innovation was the direct result of this effort to weed out inferior musicians. Kenny Clarke was the leader of Minton's house band. The drummer spurred on the soloists—and made their lives difficult—with unusual hits and accents that broke up the tempo while kicking the music into high gear. Until this time, jazz drummers generally kept up a steady beat using the foot pedal on the big bass drum. Clarke shifted the rhythm to a quick tapping of his ride cymbal. Clarke describes how he inadvertently developed this technique:

> It just happened sort of accidentally. . . . We were playing a real fast tune once with Teddy Hill—"Old Man River," I think—and the tempo was too fast to play four beats to the measure, so I began to cut the time up. But to keep the same rhythm going, I had to do it with my hand [on the cymbal], because my foot just wouldn't do it [on the bass drum]. So I started doing it

Percussionist Kenny Clarke created a new technique of revved-up cymbal riding.

with my hand, and then every once in a while I would kind of lift myself with my foot, to kind of boot my-self into it. . . . When it was over, I said, "Good God, was that ever hard." So then I began to think, and say, "Well, you know, it worked. It worked and nobody said anything, so it came out right. So that must be the way

to do it." Because I think if I had been able to do it [the old way], it would have been stiff. It wouldn't have worked.[30]

Clarke's revved-up cymbal riding soon earned him the nickname "Klook-Mop," or "Klook," a word that sounded like Clarke's drumbeat: bopklook-mop, klook-mop.

Groovin' High with Gillespie

As fate would have it, Clarke's new groove blended perfectly with the inventive trumpet playing of Dizzy Gillespie, who had come to New York to play with Cab Calloway's band during the late 1930s. Gillespie almost single-handedly invented bebop by introducing a note called a flatted fifth to the standard diatonic scale. What this meant was that in whatever scale was used as the basis for a composition, the fifth note in the scale would be played as a flat. For example, a normal C scale would be C-D-E-F-G-A-B; in this scale the G would be played as a G-flat. Using a flatted-fifth scale provides a dark, moody sound, which was called devil's music during the eighteenth century. But according to Gillespie, "With the flatted fifth I really got turned on. . . . I was excited about the progression and used it everywhere."[31]

Using this scale as a basis for his jams, Gillespie rearranged the language of jazz and became one of the most respected players of the modern era. His astounding chops were matched by his talents for composition. Gillespie wrote dozens of pieces, including "Salt Peanuts," "Groovin' High," "Blue 'n' Boogie," and "A Night in Tunisia," which became instant bebop standards. As Gridley writes,

Dizzy Gillespie's harmonic skills were startling, and he flaunted them. His phrases were full of surprises and playful changes of direction. He could precariously go in and out of keys within a single phrase, always managing to resolve the unexpected at the next chord. He often zoomed up to the trumpet's high register during the middle of a phrase and still managed to connect the melodic ideas logically. . . . And despite its complexity, his work bristled with excitement. . . . Gillespie would occasionally toy with a single note, playing it again and again, each time in a different way, creating different rhythmic patterns and using changes in loudness and tone color to achieve variety in his sound. . . . [He] could channel all his terrific energy into a ballad, using his exceptional skill with harmony, his fertile imagination, and virtuoso technique to mold a unique, personal creation.[32]

Gillespie was also responsible for introducing the Cuban sound to jazz by hiring Caribbean-born conga player Chano Pozo in 1947. Pozo did not speak a word of English, and Gillespie did not speak Spanish, but Gillespie was fascinated by the complex polyrhythms that were prominent in Cuban music. In his autobiography, Gillespie describes how Pozo taught band members polyrhythms as they traveled between gigs:

On the bus, he'd give me a drum, [bass player] Al McKibbon a drum, and he'd take a drum. Another guy would have a cowbell, and he'd give everybody a rhythm [to play]. We'd see how all the rhythms tied into one another, and everybody was playing something different. We'd be on the road in a bus, riding down the road, and we'd sing and play all down the highway. He'd teach us some of those Cuban chants and things like that. That's how I learned to play the congas.[33]

Gillespie was the first jazz bandleader to utilize these exciting rhythms on songs such as "Cubano Bop" and "Manteca." He called this new style of jazz Cubop because it combined Cuban rhythms and bebop—a marriage of Caribbean dance music and American jazz. Gillespie promoted Cubop relentlessly to show that bebop could also be dance music. The general public remained unconvinced and bebop never caught on with a wide audience.

Although Gillespie's music was largely ignored, the media could not resist his look, which became synonymous with bebop. His cheeks puffed out like balloons when he blew his horn, whose bell was bent up so that it would achieve a louder tone. He was always seen in stylish suits and wore a goatee; black, thick-rimmed "bop" glasses; and black berets. Gillespie used beatnik slang, spoke like a "hepcat," and the press loved him.

Instead of accepting the fact that the general public was alienated by his eclectic style, Gillespie promoted the music as something anyone could enjoy. During the late 1950s, he took bebop on a worldwide promotional tour, playing extensively in Japan, Europe, and South America. During the sixties, Gillespie continued to bop with small combos.

Gillespie has been credited with changing jazz in three important aspects: He created a unique trumpet style that showcased his virtuosity and redefined the possibilities of the instrument; as an ambassador of bebop to the world, he legitimized the sound as a real musical style; and Gillespie changed the dynamics between jazz musicians. Whereas many players had been afraid to reveal their secrets, even

Dizzy Gillespie is credited with inventing bebop.

playing with their backs to the others, Gillespie shared, taught, and encouraged others to reach the pinnacle of their talents.

The Bird Sings

Gillespie, the expressive emissary of bop, found his opposite in saxophonist Charlie "Bird" Parker, an introverted man of mystery. Parker was born in 1920 and grew up playing in the crossroads of music, Kansas City, Missouri. Raised on blues, ragtime, and jump, Parker pursued music

Parker's Dangerous Appetites

Charlie "Bird" Parker began shooting heroin in 1937 at the age of seventeen, and his appetite for drugs was legendary. While playing in swing bands, Parker perfected the technique of nodding on heroin (moving in and out of consciousness) behind his sunglasses, with his cheeks puffed out so it would look like he was playing. When it came time for his solo, he instructed a bandmate to jab him in the leg with a pin to wake him up.

In the mid-1940s, Parker's technical genius and emotional playing made him an instant star among the be-bop musicians playing 52nd Street in New York. Despite Parker's legendary talents, he received little attention in the media and struggled to make ends meet. Parker's abilities were finally recognized in 1949 after a successful European tour. By this time, however, his addictions were interfering with his career. He drank excessively, showed up at gigs in ragged clothes, or missed engagements altogether. His behavior was often erratic and bizarre. He was even banned from Birdland, the legendary 52nd Street club named in his honor. By 1954, addicted to cheap red wine and reduced to playing in California dive bars, Parker attempted suicide. The following year, on March 9, 1955, he died from pneumonia.

Charlie Parker rehearses in Los Angeles, California, in 1946. He was the king of bebop saxophone.

recklessly and relentlessly, jamming all night every night. Fueled by the amphetamine Benzedrine, Bird blew his sax in a high-speed cascade of notes, perfecting a style called doubling up, in which melodies were played at twice the written tempo.

By the mid-1940s, Parker was a heroin addict and an alcoholic. He was also a regular fixture at Minton's and the jazz clubs on New York's 52nd Street. He had been jamming with Gillespie since 1942, and their 1945 duet of the song

"Salt Peanuts" laid out the future of bebop in its breakneck melodies. Giddins describes Parker's genius:

> Charlie Parker was like a prophet when he first came on the scene, right at the end of the Second World War.... [His music] was explosive, out of nowhere.... It was shocking, the way Louis Armstrong was shocking in the 1920s. I mean where did this come from, this speed, the velocity, the excitement, the exhilaration? [It's] melody, but it's played so fast, and with such joy and such exhilaration that it totally revolutionized the music. . . . It's a magical thing and it's only happened relatively few times in the history of western civilization where a musician comes along and can completely transmute [change] the music.[34]

Between 1945 and 1955, Parker was the king of bebop saxophone, with a legion of admirers within the jazz community. Unfortunately, he received little critical acclaim in the mainstream media. Whereas Gillespie danced, sang, and appealed to a large audience, Parker haunted the dingy clubs of New York, toting his alto saxophone in a paper bag tied up with rubber bands. He was sometimes mistaken for a hobo until he took out his battered horn and began to play. Then, with almost superhuman concentration, Bird let fly with a burst of notes while appearing to sit stock-still behind his sunglasses.

Unfortunately, many jazz musicians thought that they could play like Bird if they took heroin too. By the mid-fifties dozens of jazz's greatest players descended into addiction. Parker himself struggled mightily before dying in 1955 at the age of thirty-four. The drugs and alcohol had taken their toll: The doctor who examined Bird's lifeless body thought he was looking at a man in his sixties.

Monk Creates a New Melody

Along with Parker and Gillespie, another important piece of the bebop puzzle was the pianist with the unusual name of Thelonious Sphere Monk. (He often joked that with the middle name of "Sphere" no one would ever call him a square, a jazz term for uncool or unhip.) Monk, born in

North Carolina in 1917 and raised in New York City, was a regular in the jazz scene, joining Clarke's house band at Minton's around 1940.

Like Gillespie, Monk was a composer whose characteristic tunes, such as "Straight No Chaser" and "Round Midnight," became bebop standards. When he tickled out the bebop on his piano keys, Monk specialized in accenting melodies in odd places and ending musical phrases with unexpected notes in a surprising flourish. In technical

Thelonious Monk— seen at the piano with fellow jazz musician Howard McGhee—was known for his intellectually complex compositions.

Bop and the Beat Generation

During the 1950s, a movement emerged among mostly white nonconformists who called themselves beatniks or the beat generation. Beat authors included Jack Kerouac, Allen Ginsberg, and William Burroughs. As literary critic Mike Janssen explains, the renowned beat writers were inspired by the bebop jazz played by Charlie Parker, Dizzy Gillespie, and Thelonious Monk:

The word *beat* was primarily . . . a slang term meaning down and out, or poor and exhausted. Kerouac went on to twist the meaning of the term "beat" to serve his own purposes, explaining that it meant [bliss or] "beatitude, not beat up. You feel this. You feel it in a beat, in jazz real cool jazz."

The Beat authors borrowed many other terms from the jazz/hipster slang of the '40s, peppering their works with words such as "square," "cats," "nowhere," and "dig." But jazz meant much more than just a vocabulary to the Beat writers. . . .

[The writers] used the principal ideas of bebop playing and applied it to prose and poetry writing, creating a style sometimes called "bop prosody." Beat prose, especially that of Jack Kerouac, is characterized by a style submerged in the stream of consciousness, words blurted out in vigorous bursts, rarely revised and often sparsely punctuated for lines and lines. . . . Ginsberg called this improvisational technique applied to writing "composing on the tongue," and it was used in one way or another by many of the Beat writers.

Mike Janssen. "Jazz." Literary Kicks, 2011. www.litkicks .com/Jazz.

terms described by writer Kenny Mathieson, Monk played "highly original harmonic progressions, dissonant intervals and oblique, angular rhythms."[35] Monk was famed for his use of flatted third chords, also called half-diminished chords, which leaves the music sounding unresolved. Monk's compositions were intellectually complex, but he also wove humor into his music. For example, in the middle of the bebop number "Sweet and Lovely," Monk plays the traditional ditty "Tea for Two."

As an enigmatic master behind the keys, Monk was misunderstood, even within the bebop community. He liked unusual hats, and he would often make odd little dances around his grand piano. These steps looked foolish to some, but in the process Monk was actually conducting the band, showing them the rhythm.

Monk demonstrated that great music is not just the notes played but the notes that are not played. He often left silent spaces in his compositions, causing some who were used to the rapid-fire riffs of Gillespie and Parker to assume Monk could not play very well. But as jazz pianist Laurent de Wilde explains,

[Monk] taught the science of the maximum economy in the choice of the notes making up a chord. Why play three when two were enough! And that's another torture for whomever tries to reproduce Monk's music: you always think you're hearing more notes than he's actually playing.[36]

Monk was never easy to understand. Many times he was totally introverted and refused to communicate with anyone. When he did speak, his convoluted and eccentric pronouncements were understood by few. During the late 1940s and 1950s Monk struggled professionally, but he was suddenly elevated to celebrity status in 1957 by a crowd of young nonconformists called beatniks who appreciated his unique brand of music.

Monk toured extensively throughout the sixties and early seventies, but he retired suddenly in 1973, suffering from mental illness. He spent the rest of his life in seclusion, but his career proved one remarkable fact about his music: It was born fully formed, and from the time he began playing in the late forties until his retirement more than twenty-five years later, he saw no need to alter his style. As the great pianist himself said, "I wanted to play my own chords. I wanted to create and invent."[37]

The Birth of Modern Jazz

By the early fifties, bebop was the predominant style of jazz, blasting out of clubs from coast to coast. In addition to the sounds of Klook-Mop, Gillespie, Bird, and Monk, the music could be heard in the recordings of sax players Dexter Gordon, Stan Getz, and Sonny Rollins; in the drumming of Max Roach; in the piano styles of Bud Powell and Billy Taylor; in the guitar playing of Barney Kessel; and the arrangements of Gil Evans.

Although the beboppers were never highly successful in the commercial sense, these jazz musicians blew a cool, wild, and free sound whose spirit seemed to be lacking in other aspects of American life during the 1950s. For this reason, bebop was the sound preferred by hepcats (players or fans of 1940s–1950s jazz), beatniks, and nonconformists who faced discrimination and prejudice in their daily lives. With fast-paced changes, complex rhythms and melodies, and improvised virtuosity, bop profoundly influenced American culture and spawned several styles, such as free jazz, cool jazz, and hard bop.

CHAPTER 4

The Cool and the Hard

In the late 1940s, as bebop blasted from clubs in New York, Chicago, and Los Angeles, traditionalist jazz critics were worried. They feared that fast-paced, dissonant, polyrhythmic sound represented "the death of jazz."[38] Such a dire statement might be seen today as overly dramatic, but bebop was radical enough to inspire a rebellion against the style. While jazz had always been criticized by more conservative elements of society, this time the challengers were from within the jazz community.

In the early 1950s, musicians, reviewers, and jazz writers split into factions. One group rejected the "hot" sounds of bebop to support cool jazz, which was influenced by swing and classical music. Songs were short and peppy, and listeners found them melodious and inviting. Cool jazz was played by musicians who were "cool" in the sense of being in control, poised, unhurried, and unruffled. The easy-listening sound was popular in laid-back, sunny California where it was known as West Coast jazz, a style largely played by white musicians.

"Real Jazz"

The second faction in the post-bebop world was not ready to relax. Back in New York, jazz players continued to experiment. Tired of playing hyperactive bebop, they created a new sound called hard bop. Hard bop is marked by long solos, and a soulful bluesy sound driven by a strong R&B (rhythm and blues) rhythm. In the 1950s, saxophonist John Coltrane exemplified the hard bop sound with his hour-long solos. During landmark jams, Coltrane created repetitive musical themes, explored them in various tempos and degrees of abstraction, and slowly built to loud, moving crescendos.

With cool jazz and hard bop moving in different directions, musicians, critics, and fans split into two camps. Each claimed that the style they preferred was "real jazz"[39] while the other sound was not. Even as the battles grew more heated in the mid-1950s, the popularity of jazz was sinking like a stone and drowned out by the sound of rock and roll. Performers such as Elvis Presley, Chuck Berry, Buddy Holly, and Jerry Lee Lewis conquered the radio and record business. With rock music dominating the airwaves, the arguments over hard bop and cool jazz were happening among the diminishing number of people who still cared about the direction of jazz.

The Birth of Cool

Of the two styles, there is little doubt that the catchy, accessible songs of cool jazz composers were more popular and commercially successful. Cool jazz got its start at the end of the 1940s when pianist Claude Thornhill toured the country with a large dance band. This group featured instruments more commonly found in a symphony orchestra including French horns, bassoons, and tubas. In 1948, the band's arranger, Gil Evans, seized on the idea of using the unique tones of these instruments in a modern jazz setting. Evans shared his idea of a lighter, more orchestral sounding jazz with the twenty-two-year-old Miles Davis. Together they created a seminal new sound.

Davis was born in 1926 and grew up in East St. Louis, Illinois. At eighteen, he was accepted by Julliard School, the prestigious performing arts conservatory in New York City. Davis honed his chops playing with Charlie Parker dur-

Miles Davis Creates a New Sound

Music journalist Richard Williams explains how the cool jazz sound on the Miles Davis album Birth of the Cool *differed from the bebop music of a previous era:*

> [When] bebop came along, although its music was sophisticated and its hipster performers proud of their cool façade, it was essentially a hot music, built on the impact created by dizzying speed of thought and execution. . . . The Miles Davis Nonet [nine-piece band] changed all that. Its sonorities were pure, its voicings open, the cadence of its music calm and smooth. Davis later said he had instructed [arrangers Bill] Evans and [saxophonist Gerry] Mulligan to create a band whose horns replicated the range of a choir: soprano (trumpet), alto (alto saxophone and French horn), tenor (trombone), baritone (baritone saxophone), and bass (tuba). André Hodeir, the French composer and critic, described the nonet as a "chamber orchestra," and saw the inclusion of the French horn as symbolizing an implicit rejection of the hot [bebop] tradition. The lack of duplication of voices and the individual players' preferences for comparatively light timbres gave the sound of the ensemble an airy clarity that immediately set it apart from everything previously heard in jazz. . . . Unlike bebop, this wasn't confrontational music. Not only did it not care if you didn't like it, it affected not even to notice.

Richard Williams. *The Blue Moment*. New York: W.W. Norton & Company, 2011, p. 51.

ing the mid-1940s but soon moved on to pursue a solo career. In the late 1940s, Evans wrote songlike arrangements that meshed perfectly with Davis's sweet trumpet tone and lyrical improvisations. The music was recorded in a series of sessions at Capitol Records between 1949 and 1950. Davis recorded with a nine-piece band, the Miles Davis Nonet, made up of bebop musicians. The band included drummer Kenny Clarke, trombonist J.J. Johnson, alto saxophonist Lee Konitz, baritone saxophonist Gerry Mulligan, pianist John Lewis, bassist Al McKibbon, and others. Some of the cool jazz songs produced by the nonet were compiled on the album *Birth of the Cool* released in an abbreviated form in 1954 and a more complete version three years later.

Miles Davis, Lee Konitz, and Gerry Mulligan (left to right) record Birth of the Cool *at Capitol Records in New York City in 1949.*

Birth of the Cool features Davis's smooth riffs over relaxed, subdued background arrangements, which give the music a large orchestral sound. Two of the songs, "Boplicity" and "Moon Dreams" provided a model texture on which the entire cool jazz sound was based. Giddins says the nonet provides "big, cloud-like harmonies where all the instruments

would come together in these huge chords that just seemed to float in the air."[40] Davis's solos were shorter than those of a typical bebop song and the cool sound was not as loud or brassy. Instead, the music was highly organized, and the ensemble sound was emphasized. Davis later described his cool playing style during this period:

> I think what they really meant [by cool] was a soft sound. . . . Not penetrating too much. To play soft you have to relax. . . . You don't delay the beat, but you might play a [group of notes] that sounds delayed. . . . I always wanted to play with a light sound, because I could think better when I played that way.[41]

The musical style behind the mild tempos and whimsical sounds of *Birth of the Cool* is known as modal jazz. While the music sounds simple and natural, the definition of modal scales is complex. Unlike older jazz styles, modal jazz is not based on a series of repetitive chord progressions. Instead a modal song might hold a single chord for an extended period, which gives the music a sort of droning quality. Depending on the type of modal scale used, the music might sound happy, serious, sad, or celestial. Several best-selling pop songs are based on modal scales, including Michael Jackson's "Thriller," the Beatles' "Eleanor Rigby" and the Red Hot Chili Peppers' "Californication."

Birth of the Cool did not generate big sales, but over the years it became Davis's best-selling album. Today it is revered as a cool jazz classic. Many of the musicians in the nonet continued to pursue the cool jazz style, and modal jazz influenced numerous artists in later years. Meanwhile, Davis abandoned cool jazz almost as soon as he pioneered it—always seeking a new and different sound.

The West Coast's Cool School

The cool sound moved west when Evans and Mulligan moved to Los Angeles after working with Davis in New York. The two put together a group with Chet Baker, whose trumpet tone often resembled Davis's moody, cool sound. With a bass player and drummer, Mulligan gave the cool sound a new flavor by adding elements of New Orleans jazz, swing, and bop. As documentary filmmaker Geoffrey C. Ward writes, "The quartet's sound was rollicking, breezy, and good-humored, inviting to those who found bebop forbidding."[42]

The move west gave cool jazz an unexpected commercial push. As fate would have it, a reporter from *Time* heard the Gerry Mulligan Quartet at a Los Angeles club called the Haig and wrote a glowing article about the sound. *Time* called the music unique and even compared it to works by eighteenth century baroque composer Johann Sebastian Bach. The positive review prompted Los Angeles radio stations to play the quartet's cool jazz songs such as "Walkin' Shoes" and "Line for Lyons." Although not as danceable as swing, the music provided enough of a beat that people could shake their heads and tap their feet. Before long, Mulligan and Baker were national jazz stars, and the press dubbed their sound the West Coast cool school.

Meanwhile, other California musicians began to experiment with the new sound. Among them were sax player Jimmy Giuffre, flutist and alto saxophonist Bud Shank, drummer Shelly Manne, and trumpeter Shorty Rogers. Manne described the goals of the cool school musicians:

Chet Baker was a star of the West Coast cool school.

> What we wanted to do . . . was write some new kind of material for jazz musicians, where the solos and the improvisations became part of the whole, and you couldn't tell where the writing ended and the improvisations began. . . . [It] was lighter, maybe a little more "laid-back."[43]

The West Coast cool school was not for everybody, however. Almost all of the major jazz magazines, including *Down Beat*, were based in New York. The East Coast critics considered West Coast cool lightweight and unimaginative, more of a movie sound track for the sunny California lifestyle than a serious art form. The record-buying public—which cared little about such matters—loved the music because of its easygoing tone and accessible melodies. In 1955, *Down Beat* readers voted Baker the best trumpet player in the country.

Brubeck Takes Five

While the Mulligan quartet popularized the cool sound among jazz fans, another California musician was writing modern jazz that appealed to a large mainstream audience. Dave Brubeck, born in 1920, was raised on the classical music of Mozart, Bach, and Beethoven. His mother, a classical piano teacher, steered him toward a music career. At college he listened to the experimental twentieth-century classical works of Arnold Schoenberg and studied music with French composer Darius Milhaud.

In 1951, Brubeck formed the Dave Brubeck Quartet with alto saxophonist Paul Desmond, drummer Joe Dodge, and bassist Bob Bates. The sound of this group epitomized the West Coast cool school. Brubeck's light touch on the piano matched Desmond's lyrical style of improvisation. Shunning the rapid-fire delivery of beboppers, Desmond was known for his ability to pick a few sweet notes. As Brubeck remembers,

> There are so few guys that can play with the purity Paul had . . . people who can develop a theme and not play a million notes, but rather choice notes. . . . Paul was picking those notes with a great combination of intellect and concern for the purity of his sound and he wasn't out to dazzle anyone.[44]

Despite this modest assessment, the Dave Brubeck Quartet did dazzle audiences—and these were not typical jazz crowds. The group avoided smoky, dark jazz clubs and instead booked gigs on college campuses. The quartet toured the country in Brubeck's station wagon with the string bass tied to the roof. At the time, playing at colleges was a controversial move. As Brubeck says, "Most [schools] in the United States still wouldn't let you play jazz, even in a practice room."[45] Nonetheless, middle-class college students loved Brubeck's modern jazz sound.

In another bold move, Brubeck released the first live jazz album, *Jazz at Oberlin*, recorded at the Ohio college. When this was released in 1953, it sold so well that the band was signed by the prestigious Columbia Records. When a second live album, *Jazz Goes to College*, was released in 1954, it sold more than one hundred thousand copies, a huge number for a jazz record during that era. Such record-setting sales gained the notice of *Time*, whose editors put Brubeck on the magazine's cover—making him the first jazz musician to ever be so honored.

Throughout the fifties, the Dave Brubeck Quartet was the defining sound of West Coast jazz for most Americans. Yet Brubeck's group continued to innovate. In 1959, the quartet released "Take Five," a song recorded in the 5/4 time signature as opposed to the standard 4/4 of most cool jazz. The song's unusual but memorable rhythm propelled it to the top of the charts. "Take Five" became the first jazz record in history to sell more than a million copies. The success of this innovative song inspired the Brubeck group to experiment with other unusual time signatures, such as 7/8 and 9/8.

Davis Grooves with Hard Bop

The music played by Brubeck and his contemporaries did not appeal to everyone. Although the laid-back West Coast cool jazz sold millions of records to suburban audiences, it "went largely unnoticed by [African American] musicians in the East, except as an irritant,"[46] according to jazz journalist Joe Goldberg. Instead, black jazz musicians in New York continued to push the boundaries with their music, playing long, winding hard bop jams for their own gratification rather than the approval of the young, white, "square" audiences.

Hard bop is bebop taken to a higher level of complexity. The sound often has a hard-driving beat, blues-based improvisations, and passionate, emotional solos. As Gridley writes, "In contrast to the polite, chamber music feeling

"Take Five" by the Dave Brubeck Quartet was the first jazz record in history to sell more than a million copies.

Art Blakey's Drum Style

As the leader of the Jazz Messengers for more than four decades, the drumming of Art Blakey is the rock-solid foundation of hard bop. Blakey's groundbreaking style is explored on the Public Broadcasting Service (PBS) website:

Although Blakey discourages comparison of his own music with African drumming, he adopted several African devices after his visit in 1948–9, including rapping on the side of the drum and using his elbow on the tom-tom to alter the pitch. Later he organized recording sessions with multiple drummers, including some African musicians and pieces. His much-imitated trademark, the forceful closing of the hi-hat on every second and fourth beat, has been part of his style since 1950–51.

Blakey is a major figure in modern jazz and an important stylist in drums. From his earliest recording session . . . particularly in his historic sessions with [Thelonious] Monk in 1947, he exudes power and originality, creating a dark cymbal sound punctuated by frequent loud snare and bass drum accents in triplets or cross-rhythms. A loud and domineering drummer, Blakey also listens and responds to his soloists. His contribution to jazz as a discoverer and molder of young talent over three decades is no less significant than his very considerable innovations on his instrument.

The drumming of Art Blakey, leader of the Jazz Messengers, was the foundation of hard bop.

"Art Blakey." PBS, 2011. www.pbs.org/jazz/biography/artist_id_blakey_art.htm.

projected by much of the West Coast style, some hard bop projected a funky, earthy feeling."[47]

As he had earlier done with cool jazz, Miles Davis pioneered the hard bop sound, this time on the 1954 album *Bags' Groove*. The album featured Kenny Clarke on drums, Monk on piano, Horace Silver on bass and piano, Sonny Rollins on tenor sax, and Milt Jackson on vibraphone. Davis's solos were brassy, the melodies were catchy, and the walking bass beat gave songs a toe-tapping rhythm and blues (R&B) feel. Hasse describes how players achieved the new sound:

> The hard-bop musicians used much the same vocabulary and grammar as bebop, but they turned the language to somewhat different ends to suit the demands of a new decade. They relaxed the tempos that had often made bebop a breathtaking steeplechase, and they simplified the knotty melodies that had delighted Parker and Dizzy Gillespie. In so doing, the hard-bop players brought back an earthy soulfulness that had receded during the boppers' quest for more "serious" recognition. This soulfulness had its roots in the ecstasy of church and gospel music, which provided the first listening experience for many black musicians, and which permeates such hard-bop classics.[48]

The Messengers Deliver

After playing with Davis, pianist and composer Silver went on to become a leading proponent of hard bop. Joining forces with drummer Art Blakey, Silver put together a quintet called the Jazz Messengers in 1955. The Messengers put a friendly face on hard bop, mixing improvised horn sounds, an infectious walking bass line, and Blakey's boisterous, rocking beat. Silver later described the band's attitude:

> We weren't trying to do nothing but just cook, swing, make it happen. We called Art "Little Dynamo" he had so much drive, power, swing. . . . Art was loud— robust, you know? . . . You had to match up so as not [to] sound like a weakling or a fool.[49]

The music of the Messengers appealed to listeners who could relate to the blues- and swing-driven sounds not found in bebop. After the release of the 1955 live album *At the Café Bohemia*, the Jazz Messengers' singles were blasting out of jukeboxes in African American neighborhoods coast to coast.

The Jazz Messengers continued making music for decades with an ever-changing cast of players. Many Messengers' musicians went on to become stars in their own right, including trumpet players Donald Byrd, Freddie Hubbard, Chuck Mangione, Woody Shaw, and Wynton Marsalis; pianists Keith Jarrett and JoAnne Brackeen; and saxophonist Wayne Shorter.

Jazz Giant Coltrane

The sound of hard bop was defined by the rollicking drums, the brassy trumpet, and the expressive sound of the wailing tenor sax. Some of the greatest tenor sax players of the 1950s, including Sonny Rollins and Dexter Gordon, cut their chops on hard bop. Gordon was almost superhuman, blowing long strings of rich, smoky riffs without taking a breath.

John Coltrane was one of the many tenor players influenced by Gordon. Coltrane, or Trane, went on to forever change the way the tenor saxophone was played. Carl Woideck explains in *The John Coltrane Companion:*

> John Coltrane's significance in jazz history—as a saxophonist, composer, and bandleader—is comparable only with a handful of other figures. His improvisational and compositional contributions were so broad that his music influenced players on all instruments, not just saxophone. More than thirty years after his death, young jazz musicians several generations removed from Coltrane are still inspired by his dedication to music, pursuit of musical knowledge, and pursuit of instrumental technique.[50]

Coltrane played bebop with Dizzy Gillespie during the late forties and early fifties and hard bop with the Miles Davis Quintet between 1955 and 1957. Throughout much of this time Coltrane was a heroin addict, but he gave up drugs, alcohol, and cigarettes in 1957 to study Eastern religions, meditation, and yoga. This spiritual awakening led

him to study the modal music of India, particularly ragas, which are partly improvised. The scales, melodies, and rhythmic patterns of raga are intended to create different moods. Some ragas are exciting, some deeply hypnotic. As Coltrane said, "Most of what we play in jazz has the feeling of . . . raga."[51] These songs, which combined technical skill,

Saxophonist John Coltrane continues to influence musicians decades after his death.

Coltrane's Long Solos

Drummer Jimmy Cobb describes playing with John Coltrane, or Trane, whose long saxophone solos were legendary:

Coltrane would play all night, and come off the intermission and go somewhere and play—stand in a corner or something. You know, Miles [Davis] had to make him stop, because he would play an hour solo himself, and we were only supposed to be on the [bandstand] for forty minutes or something. He had incredible chops—he couldn't stop. Miles used to say, "Man, look, why don't you play twenty-seven choruses instead of twenty-eight?" Coltrane would say, "I get involved in this thing and I don't know how to stop." Miles once suggested, "Try taking the saxophone out of your mouth." . . .

We were playing at the Sutherland in Chicago once, when Trane was just finishing one of his thirty-minute solos. I was feeling so tired of playing so long a drumstick flew out of my hand and whipped by Trane's head, just missing him. When we finished the set, I told him, "I'm sorry, man, it just slipped out of my hand." He said, "I thought you finally threw something at me for playing so long."

Quoted in Bill Crow. *Jazz Anecdotes: Second Time Around.* New York: Oxford University Press, 2005, p. 361.

musical innovation, and a deep spiritual feel, strongly influenced Coltrane's music and all those who emulated him.

Sheets of Sound

Like Davis, Coltrane was not afraid to experiment. He pioneered such techniques as blowing several notes at once, bending his tones in a bluesy manner, and playing extended solos. These techniques, however, were controversial. One critic called Coltrane's music "anti-jazz"; another critic, Ira Gitler, famously defined it as "sheets of sound."[52]

Coltrane's landmark solo albums, such as *Blue Trane* (1957), *Soul Trane* (1958), and *Giant Steps* (1960), made Coltrane an international star. By the early sixties, Trane was recording his sheets of sound on at least one album a year. But it was his jazzed-up soprano saxophone version of the Rodgers and Hammerstein song "My Favorite Things," from the hit musical play *The Sound of Music*, which brought Coltrane his biggest success in 1961.

This unlikely choice for groundbreaking jazz became Coltrane's signature tune. Weighing in at an astounding fourteen minutes (in an era when the average pop tune was under three minutes), the song allows the sax player to showcase his talents. Coltrane's fingers run up and down the keys as he dances around the melody, swooping and throwing in warbling trills. He alternately makes the sax sing sweetly and then screech, like a bird on the attack. Coltrane's jazzed-up version of "My Favorite Things" brought him widespread notice from the general public, which might not have heard his music otherwise.

Coltrane continued to release albums throughout the sixties, some experimenting with pop melodies, others taking on musical paths of Indian ragas and free-form experimentation. In 1967, the jazz world was stunned when the sax master died of liver cancer at the age of forty-one. Fortunately for listeners, Coltrane had dozens of finished albums, which were gradually released years after his death. Wynton Marsalis explains why Coltrane's music continued to sound very alive decades after his death:

> [The] thing that's always in John Coltrane is the lyrical shout of the preacher in the heat and full fury of attempting to transform the congregation. And that's the source of John Coltrane's power. We talk about sheets of sound . . . all the different things that he did. He . . . brought a lot of things into his music but the center of his music is that Sunday morning pulpit revival church meeting holler and shout. And more than any other jazz musician, he has that in his sound.[53]

Although Coltrane has been identified as one of the most influential jazz artists of any age, few were able to follow in his footsteps. Nonetheless, he inspired musicians to take chances, devote themselves to their music, and continue to experiment in the face of criticism.

Jazz for the Soul

Coltrane's musical voice was one of the unifying sounds during an era when jazz was becoming fragmented. Even as cool jazz fans argued with hard bop lovers over which style was better, new sounds emerged that further divided the jazz community. The musical changes were propelled by new instruments taking the lead, steering jazz away from its traditional horn-based sound. The style known as soul jazz was driven by the electric Hammond organ, traditionally played with gospel church choirs.

Soul jazz incorporated elements of other popular African American music styles of the 1950s including R&B, gospel, urban blues, and rock and roll. By the late 1950s, Jimmy Smith established the Hammond organ as a legitimate jazz instrument on finger-snapping songs such as "Back at the Chicken Shack." This song featured Kenny Burrell on electric guitar, another important instrument in the soul jazz sound.

Whether the style was cool, hard bop, or soul jazz, each school had its own devotees and detractors. However, the disputes and debates over the direction of jazz were largely ignored by the general public and the media. As musician and jazz critic Ted Gioia writes, when musicians and fans divided into different camps, jazz "rapidly became a subculture on the fringes of the entertainment industry."[54] The death of jazz had been predicted for several decades, but the musical style refused to die. Within a few years, a new generation raised on rock would propel jazz back into the mainstream, while the genius of 1950s music by Davis, Coltrane, and Brubeck would be revered well into the twenty-first century.

CHAPTER 5

Free Jazz and Fusion

Between 1945 and 1967, John Coltrane invented and reinvented his sound. Although his various recordings are categorized as bebop or hard bop, oftentimes Trane played music that could not be classified. His improvisations were liberated from traditional musical rules such as melody, rhythm, key, and preset chord progressions. In the 1960s that sound came to be identified as free jazz, an anything-goes, rolling, tumbling sound described as turbulent and frenzied. The chaotic free jazz style can sound like musicians battling one another with riffs, rather than playing a song together. Free jazz is a far different sound than anything ever imagined by Louis Armstrong or even Dizzy Gillespie. Free is considered by some purists to be the ultimate in jazz expression.

Shrieks, Squawks, Wails, and Gurgles

While Coltrane played free style, alto saxophonist Ornette Coleman is considered one of the founding fathers of the free jazz school of musical expression. Unlike Coltrane, who was considered a monster talent with amazing chops, Coleman was valued for emotional expression rather than his technical skills on the instrument.

Coleman concentrated on wringing a wide array of

unusual sounds from the sax. As Gridley writes, Coleman "earned a reputation for more extensive manipulations of pitch and tone quality. . . . Ultra-high register playing [called altissimo], plus shrieks, squawks, wails, gurgles, and squeals were common. . . . Sustained notes alternated with screeches and moans."[55] Sometimes Coleman abandoned his brass saxophone and instead played a plastic toy sax that emitted an unearthly screech. This innovation inspired other free jazz groups, such as the Art Ensemble of Chicago, to employ unusual noisemakers such as whistles, gongs, toy instruments, and bells. Coleman later taught himself to play violin and trumpet, which he added to his free-flowing, formless jams.

Coleman based his work on a concept called harmelodics, which he invented. In harmelodics every element of a composition—harmony, melody, rhythm, and tempo—are considered equal. Instead of a melody dominating one part of a song, with the beat or harmony emphasized in another, all sounds can happen all at once and with uniform volume. The essence of the harmelodics musical theory can be heard on Coleman's 1961 album, appropriately titled *Free Jazz*. Each one of the two stereo channels on the record has a separate quartet improvising wildly for thirty-seven minutes. This means eight musicians in two separate bands are playing different music at the same time. As Gioia writes, *Free Jazz* broke all the rules.

> [It] took on overtones of a spectacle, serving as a jazz equivalent of those battles royal favored by television wrestling [fans], brutish encounters in which a number of well-toned bodies engage in simultaneous, extemporaneous sparring. . . . Churning and seething, sounds ricocheting between two quartets, a relentless energy [permeated] the music.[56]

Leaps into Space

If Coleman was a free jazz wrestler, the classically trained virtuoso pianist Cecil Taylor was its intellectual scholar. Taylor drew not only from classical symphonies but from many African American musical styles. In a single song, which might last more than two hours, Taylor could use call-and-

Coleman's Musical Theory

The free jazz of Ornette Coleman often sounds like two groups in battle. On Coleman's 1961 album, Free Jazz, *one quartet blasts from the left channel of the stereo, while a different jam booms from the right. A listener wearing headphones has the unique, and possibly uncomfortable, experience of hearing two different songs playing at the same time. Coleman based his free jazz concept on a musical theory he developed called harmelodics, a merging of the words harmony and melody. This far-out musical concept, in which all musicians are free to improvise as long and loud as they want, was explained in somewhat abstract terms by Coleman in 1982:*

> Harmelodics is a system that will allow the person to lead or to extract any part of [a musical] idea in order to enhance the particular philosophy they feel will allow the composition to develop . . . [for the betterment of] the total sound. In other words, Harmelodics is a philosophy based upon all forms of concepts or ideas being equal. . . . The time, the rhythm, the speed, the harmonics are all equal.

Quoted in David Meltzer, ed. *Writing Jazz.* San Francisco: Mercury House, 1999, pp. 239–240.

response techniques, blues improvisations, boogie-woogie bass runs, and bebop phrases. These components might not be obvious to a casual listener. Taylor encoded them in clusters of sound or only hinted at them with abstract riffs that flowed and gushed out of his fingers at a breakneck pace. His playing was physical as well as musical, and he produced crescendo after crescendo of atonal dissonance until listeners were exhausted. Taylor described the music speeding from his keyboard as "the magical lifting of one's spirits into a state of trance. . . . I try to imitate on the piano the leaps into space a dancer makes."[57]

Taylor's demanding music was hardly popular. In 1962, he only played a handful of gigs each year and was often forced to support himself as a dishwasher or short-order cook. However, Taylor's 1966 album *Unit Structures* helped him gain recognition among a wider audience, and in the early 1970s he released several critically acclaimed albums of his solo concerts including *Indent* (1973) and *Silent Tongues* (1974).

Mingus's Thrumming

Bassist Charles Mingus was another jazz pioneer who drew freely from African American roots music. Bass players and drummers traditionally guide the beat and tempo of a band, and Mingus's jazz style was inspired by the rock-solid swinging sounds of gospel and R&B. While Mingus achieved fame during the free jazz era, his music was unto itself and beyond classification. As arts journalist Dirk Sutro writes:

> Seldom has a jazz musician combined such intricate songwriting with loose, inspired performances by all the players. Raw, squealing horns skitter over Mingus's low, rumbling bass and seem to capture the energy and uncertainty of [the 1960s] era of rapid change in America. . . . The album *Mingus Mingus Mingus Mingus Mingus* . . . from 1963 opens with Mingus's bass calling out in a deep, moaning voice. Here again, and throughout this collection, are Mingus's dense, dark arrangements of horns; his playing is extremely assured as he drives his band relentlessly with a thrumming undercurrent.[58]

A Collision of Sound

Led by the jazz music of Mingus, Coleman, and Taylor, the second half of the 1960s unfolded as a time of unbridled experimentation in all styles of music. It was an era when bands

Cecil Taylor, performing at the Newport Jazz Festival in Rhode Island in 1957, is a classically trained virtuoso pianist.

Jazz Meets Rock

While rock music influenced jazz in the 1960s, jazz also influenced rock musicians. Jazz record producer Bill Milkowski explains:

Frank Zappa's contribution to [the] cross-fertilization process that was occurring between rock and jazz in 1966 cannot be overstated. On his first album [with the Mothers of Invention]—the highly experimental underground classic—*Freak Out!* . . . Zappa listed the names of jazz greats Cecil Taylor, Roland Kirk, Eric Dolphy, and Charles Mingus . . . as important influences on his music. . . .

The year 1967 was pivotal for the courtship of rock and jazz. In its July issue that year, the staunch jazz publication *Down Beat* announced that it would expand its coverage to encompass rock. . . . Jimi Hendrix melded electronic feedback to Mitch Mitchell's swinging ride cymbal work on "Third Stone from the Sun," arguably Jimi's "jazziest" tune and a centerpiece on his . . . debut, *Are You Experienced.* . . . Back in the States, [Byrds' leader] Roger McGuinn had John Coltrane's "sheets of sound" in mind when he recorded his droning guitar parts to the Byrds' [number-one hit] "Eight Miles High," while Lou Reed had Ornette Coleman in mind when he cut his avant-punk guitar solo to "I Heard Her Call My Name" from the Velvet Underground's *White Light/White Heat.* . . . Clearly, the two worlds were on a collision course.

Quoted in Bill Kirchner. *The Oxford Companion to Jazz.* New York: Oxford University Press, 2000, p. 505.

incorporated dozens of different instruments and musical styles into their songs. Traditional classical instruments such as cellos, flutes, oboes, and French horns were used as accompaniments by rock groups such as the Beatles. Bands like Blood, Sweat & Tears recorded a type of rock-jazz fusion with saxophones, trumpets, congas, and trombones. Electric guitars and amplifiers expanded the vocabulary of music, along with sound effect pedals such as the wah-wah, the distortion heavy fuzz tone, and the phase shifter (which produces a subtle swirling sound). Jerry Garcia, lead guitarist for the Grateful Dead, imitated Coltrane's sax solos on his electric guitar. The Dead and other rock groups, like Cream featuring Eric Clapton, popularized jazz-like jamming in which long, improvised guitar solos were melded with wild bass riffs and African-style polyrhythmic drumming.

By the end of the 1960s the music business was almost totally dominated by the new sounds of soul and rock and roll. The brave and bold jazz experimentation by 1950s-era players sounded almost quaint in comparison to the psychedelic cacophony heard on mainstream radio stations. As jazz critic Peter Keepnews explains:

> Listeners who a few years earlier might have gravitated toward jazz had by the late sixties discovered in the music of the Beatles, Bob Dylan, Jimi Hendrix, and others not just the [primitive] excitement that had always been at the heart of rock-and-roll but also a considerable degree of musical sophistication—as well as lyrics that [addressed the growing] . . . sense that the old social and political order was crumbling and some sort of utopian revolution was in the air. It was hard for jazz, a primarily instrumental music with roots stretching back to the early days of the century, to compete with a music that literally spoke to its listeners about the concerns and emotions of the moment.[59]

To add to its problems, jazz remained divided against itself. Players from the previous generation believed that the squeaking, honking sound of free jazz did not even deserve to be called music. Miles Davis held Ornette Coleman in total disdain, commenting, "Hell, just listen to what he writes and how he plays . . . the man is all screwed up inside."[60]

In this era, jazz musicians who had been famous in earlier decades struggled to find work in small clubs; others moved to Europe, where bebop, hard bop, and cool jazz were still appreciated by large audiences. But in the United

States, according to Miles Davis, "All of a sudden jazz became passé, something dead you put under a glass in the museum and study. All of a sudden rock 'n' roll was in the forefront of the media."[61]

Fusing the Music

Against this backdrop of discord within the jazz community, a new generation of jazz artists decided to ride the rock tidal wave rather than fight it. They did so by incorporating the most commercially successful elements of rock and roll into jazz music. A new form of jazz, called fusion, emerged from this meeting of musical genres.

Fusion musicians discarded the traditional saxophone and trumpet configuration of earlier jazz combos. Instead they featured electric guitars, pianos, organs, and the newly introduced synthesizer keyboard, which could produce unique complex sounds or mimic other instruments such as violins and horns. The old-style stand-up bass was replaced by the electric bass guitar. Fusion drummers expanded their kits, adding bells, shakers, rattles, and other traditional Latin and African percussion instruments. Drummers also played differently, shunning the stretched and broken rhythms of free jazz in favor of the straight 4/4 rock beat.

With all of its electronic instruments and drums, jazz fusion was loud—much louder than music played with horns and string basses. Yet fusion players continued to rely on a deep knowledge of music. As jazz record producer Bill Milkowski writes: "Propelled by sheer decibels and a blistering intensity, this adventurous new [fusion] music was tempered by a sophisticated sense of harmony and theory that went well beyond the scope of most rock musicians of the day."[62]

The new style caught on among a younger generation raised on rock, and fusion record sales soared. Many of the best-selling albums were inspired by the top pop music of the day. Jazz guitarist Larry Coryell recalls, "We were in the middle of a world cultural revolution . . . and the prevailing attitude was 'Let's do something different.' . . . We loved Coltrane but we also dug the Beatles. We loved Miles but we also loved the Rolling Stones."[63]

Davis Brews a New Sound

Like previous new jazz sounds, fusion was rejected by some jazz traditionalists who called it "con-fusion."[64] But some old faces could still be found on the fusion scene. Miles

Innovative guitarist Larry Coryell performs at the Newport Jazz Festival in 1973.

Davis had been inventing new jazz styles for nearly his entire career, pioneering cool jazz and hard bop in the early years. So it was no surprise that the man who had feared jazz was passé was able to singlehandedly jump-start the fusion era in 1969 with the album *Bitches Brew.*

To record the album, Davis filled the studio with musicians who would later become a who's who of mass-market jazz fusion. They included drummers Don Alias, Lenny White, and Jack DeJohnette; percussionists Airto Moreira and Jim Riley; electric bassists Harvey Brooks and Dave Holland; saxophonist Wayne Shorter; British electric guitarist wizard John McLaughlin; and pianists Chick Corea and Joe Zawinul.

The original recording of *Bitches Brew* was a double record set with only seven songs on four sides of vinyl. The title track clocked in at more than twenty-six minutes, and at any given time up to twelve musicians might be playing on a song. The sound itself is a collection of musical phrases tossed out by the individual players rather than the traditional jazz style of musicians trading solos.

The electric keyboards and guitars on *Bitches Brew* give the music the sound of a rock band jamming. Some tracks exude a slow, textured, hypnotic, psychedelic sound, while others feature rock riffing with McLaughlin's solid guitar chords in counterpoint to piano runs. Davis often maintains his trademark moody tone, but at times his chaotic riffs seemed more inspired by the howling guitar runs of rock guitar superstar Jimi Hendrix than the smooth bop melodies of Dizzy Gillespie.

Bitches Brew was a stunning success, with fans of three musical styles—rock, jazz, and blues—pushing the sales figures toward a million. During the following six-year period when he was known as "Electric Miles," Davis recorded enough material for twenty albums, twelve of which were released. The trumpet wizard continued to forge a rock-solid fusion sound with each successive album created to cover new musical ground. Some albums, such as the 1971 movie sound track *A Tribute to Jack Johnson,* are almost straight rock albums. The 1974 *Big Fun* is a double album made up of only four long songs featuring the strong grooves and funk guitar playing of McLaughlin, who by this time was a musical legend in his own right.

McLaughlin's *Birds of Fire*

In the years before he recorded with Davis, McLaughlin worked with rock and roll players including members of the Rolling Stones and Cream. In 1971, McLaughlin formed his own band, the Mahavishnu Orchestra. McLaughlin was a devotee of the Indian spiritual adviser Sri Chinmoy, who suggested the band's name. Mahavishnu means "divine compassion, power, and justice" in Hindi.

The word *power* aptly describes McLaughlin's playing on the Mahavishnu Orchestra's 1973 album, *Birds of Fire*.

John McLaughlin, playing a double-necked guitar, and bassist Ralphe Armstrong of Mahavishnu Orchestra perform in Central Park in New York City in the 1970s.

The Mahavishnu Orchestra Rocks

In 1971, guitar virtuoso John McLaughlin formed the Mahavishnu Orchestra. The group fused free jazz to rock and roll on several albums including The Inner Mounting Flame *(1971) and* Birds of Fire *(1973). Jazz critic Gary Giddins and jazz scholar Scott DeVeaux describe the Mahavishnu Orchestra during concert performances:*

Mahavishnu Orchestra was an ideal band for the times. It played loud, fast, intensely distorted music, better suited to concert dates with [rock groups] ZZ Top and Emerson, Lake and Palmer than to the confined quarters of a jazz club. McLaughlin was out front, playing electric guitar with two necks—one with six strings, the other with twelve. With lengthy solos, playing at sledgehammer volume, McLaughlin raised the level of virtuosity associated with rock guitarists like Hendrix to a new level. Yet he was also part of a band. A typical Mahavishnu tune featured McLaughlin playing seamlessly alongside the amplified violin of Jerry Goodman, the electric keyboard of Jan Hammer (who had to be convinced that a jazz group wouldn't damage his reputation), and drummer Billy Cobham, a powerhouse who, like McLaughlin, had recently worked with Miles [Davis]. Although one observer compared Mahavishnu to "a car that could only function at 100 miles per hour," the group's inventiveness was undeniable.

Gary Giddins and Scott DeVeaux. *Jazz*. New York: W.W. Norton & Company, 2009, p. 543.

With his wah wah, fuzz tone, and phase shifter, McLaughlin changed the meaning of jazz guitar, giving it a screaming, soaring, rock and roll edge. His astounding technical abilities, honed with Davis, exerted a strong influence on rock guitarists of the era. As Gridley writes,

McLaughlin is notable for a phenomenally high level of instrumental proficiency. . . . He may also be responsible for some of the rise in musicianship which has characterized rock guitarists since 1970. Despite his being considered a jazz musician, McLaughlin used a tone which was . . . hard, not soft, cutting, not smooth, and metallic, not warm. In short, it had the color and texture preferred by rock guitarists, not jazz guitarists.[65]

McLaughlin and a revolving cast of players produced five Mahavishnu Orchestra albums before the group dissolved in 1976. The fusion records, which combined rock, Indian raga, and jazz, sold phenomenally well and charted in the Top 100 on pop music charts.

Pat Metheny's Boundless Imagination

The fusion of jazz and rock and roll opened the door to a wide array of individual interpretations as to what the new jazz style entailed. Like McLaughlin, Missouri-born Pat Metheny had his own unique musical voice, which allowed him to become a commercial success during the 1970s.

Pat Metheny was one of the most successful jazz fusion musicians in the 1980s.

Metheny was a musical prodigy who began teaching at the prestigious Berklee College of Music in Boston while still in his teens. At twenty-three he started the Pat Metheny Group with pianist Lyle Mays. Metheny's late 1970s and early 1980s albums, *American Garage* and *Offramp*, were best-sellers, moving one hundred thousand copies or more. By 1985, Metheny had recorded a dozen albums in a nine-year period, three of them receiving Grammy Award nominations.

With an easygoing sound mellowed by the phase shifter, Metheny's compositions have been described as folk-jazz, easy-listening jazz, or simply mood music. Critic Calvin Wilson describes Metheny's variable sound:

Metheny, more than many others, symbolized the flexibility of late [twentieth-] century jazz. In a typical performance, his group drew from bop, Brazilian samba, even the most out-and-out avant-garde jazz, employing virtually any stylistic and sonic element as long as it supported the musical statement being made. . . . Metheny proved an improviser of boundless imagination and energy. He also proved one of the most commercially successful jazz musicians of the 1980s, just as the fusion movement reached a larger audience than had the mainstream jazz of preceding years.[66]

Chick Corea Returns to Forever

Metheny was not the only *Bitches Brew* alumnus who promoted jazz fusion in the mainstream marketplace. Keyboardist Chick Corea, born in Massachusetts in 1941, was an international star by the early 1970s thanks to his work recording and touring with Davis. In 1972, Corea formed a highly influential band called Return to Forever with saxophonist Joe Farrell, bassist Stanley Clarke, Brazilian percussionist Airto Moreira (another Davis alumnus), and Moreira's wife, vocalist Flora Purim. The albums *Return to Forever* and *Light as a Feather* both have a unique sound, strongly influenced by the samba-flavored beat of Moreira and the soaring vocals of Purim, whose voice has a six-octave range. Today the albums, with their blend of spacey jazz piano and tropical-flavored Brazilian and Latin rhythms, are considered jazz fusion classics.

Return to Forever recorded throughout the seventies with constant changes in the lineup. Corea continued to record as a solo artist, experimenting with electronic ensembles, solo piano, classical music, and high-powered acoustic duos. Several of the pianist's compositions, such as "Spain," "La Fiesta," and "Windows," have become jazz standards.

Check the Weather Report

Joe Zawinul, another keyboard player who jammed with Miles Davis on *Bitches Brew*, was responsible for founding the group Weather Report with other Davis alumni Shorter and Moreira. With this stellar lineup, Weather

Report was one of the few jazz-fusion supergroups during the last three decades of the twentieth century. The music created by the group is a lively mix of Latin samba, African dance rhythms, beat-heavy funk, rock, and jazz improvisation.

Renowned bassist Jaco Pastorius joined Weather Report in 1976 after several years with Metheny. His melodious, phase-shifting bass guitar runs inspired a generation of bass players, as Wilson explains:

> A phenomenal technician with a boundless musical imagination, Pastorius was as capable of firing off rapid, precisely articulated bop phrases as he was of coaxing plaintive, voicelike melodies from his distinctive instrument of choice, a fretless electric bass. He spawned an army of imitators and drew raves as the instrument's most influential practitioner.[67]

During the Pastorius era, Weather Report reached its peak of fame, bringing freewheeling jam sessions to concert stages across the globe. In 1977, the album *Heavy Weather* was a best-seller, and its song "Birdland" became an instant jazz standard.

Herbie Hancock's Head Hunters

While Zawinul had only begun playing with Davis in 1969, Chicago-based pianist Herbie Hancock had been jamming with the trumpet player since 1963. During the sixties, Hancock wrote and recorded dozens of jazz standards with Davis, including "The Sorcerer," "Cantaloupe Island," and "Riot."

In 1973, Hancock recorded his masterpiece *Head Hunters*, a heavily electric jazz fusion record that quickly became the top-selling jazz album in history. The lead song on the album, "Chameleon," fuses funk and jazz, sounding more like Godfather of Soul James Brown than jazz rock. *Head Hunters* made Hancock an international superstar. In 1981, he teamed up with Corea and pianists Keith Jarrett and McCoy Tyner on the album *Chick Corea, Herbie Hancock, Keith Jarrett, McCoy Tyner,* a musical feast for lovers of acoustic jazz piano.

Marsalis's Postbop

*Wynton Marsalis
pioneered postbop,
a sort of fusion of
previous jazz styles.*

In 1981, Hancock played the Newport Jazz Festival backed by a young trumpet player named Wynton Marsalis, who quickly became an international superstar in his own right. Marsalis, a member of a legendary musical family in New Orleans that includes his saxophonist brother Branford Marsalis, pioneered a new style called neo-bop, or postbop. Marsalis based his sound on the bebop and hard bop music of an earlier generation. Although difficult to define, postbop is a sort of fusion of all previous jazz styles and can even incorporate the blues.

In 1981, Marsalis released *Wynton Marsalis,* his first album as a jazz bandleader. It was clear from this debut that Marsalis was already a major force in jazz. In the following years, Marsalis became one of the most famous young jazz musicians in the world. His later albums covered many styles, from old time New Orleans swing to bop and cool jazz. Some songs on his album were reminiscent of Davis and Coltrane, while others recalled the elegance of Ellington.

Marsalis's contributions to jazz were more than musical. When not touring or recording, he dedicated his life to promoting jazz as a respectable art form. Marsalis worked to keep the music alive by bringing it to a younger audience. He placed a premium on teaching and often met with students to conduct master classes in jazz music and trumpet playing. In 1996, he won the prestigious Peabody Award for his twenty-six-part educational series "Marsalis on Music." As a leading jazz ambassador, Marsalis was a welcome addition to the Lincoln Center Jazz for Young People program in New York. He continues to play a major role at Lincoln Center in the 2010s.

With Marsalis as the leading spokesman for jazz, a new generation was able to learn old traditions while looking to the future. His success created a demand for other post-bop "young lions" such as trumpeter Nicholas Payne and pianist Marcus Roberts. Thanks to the success of Marsalis, jazz continued to grow and evolve. Neo-bop kept jazz very much alive—and with a swinging beat that would not quit.

CHAPTER 6

Nu Jazz for New Times

The World Wide Web went online for the first time in 1993 and fueled a musical explosion. Anyone with a computer and a modem could listen to Internet radio stations or personal websites streaming a dizzying array of new sounds. With a click of the mouse, listeners could hear free jazz, Afro-Cuban dance music, Brazilian funk, French electronica, alternative rock, reggae, hip-hop, and countless other styles. Musicians and interested listeners alike could immerse themselves in music from nearly every country and culture on the planet. Jazz drummer David Moss comments on how the bombardment of musical information affects his music: "The influences are inescapable. They are just there. We can't get away from them. We hear them all the time."[68]

Jazz musicians searching for inspiration began to blend various styles, creating new ones along the way. While this exploding diversity in jazz defies a single label, Moss calls it the "music of hyphens."[69] This means that any given song might contain a hyphenated fusion of two or more styles such as bebop-free jazz or hard bop-swing-rap.

Nu and Free

The ever-changing jazz sound of the twenty-first century is sometimes called multistylistic. Others use the label new, or nu jazz, to describe music that mixes all styles of jazz with punk, funk, hip-hop, and synthesizer-based electronica. Nu jazz was at the heart of the trend toward musical diversity and the open-minded mixing of sounds that continued into the 2010s.

In previous times, a single type of jazz often defined an entire decade. Musicians who stepped outside the popular genre faced criticism and struggled with their careers. In the era of nu jazz, those boundaries came to be viewed as artificial and limiting. The nu sound was based on the idea that no single style defined jazz, and no genre was better or worse than another. This was free jazz in the truest sense. Every style was acceptable, and musicians were free to play whatever moved them at any given time.

The Irregular Rhythms of M-Base

The roots of nu jazz can be traced to Chicago alto saxophonist Steve Coleman (no relation to Ornette). Coleman was raised listening to Charlie Parker and moved to New York City in 1978 at the age of twenty-two where he landed a gig playing free jazz with Cecil Taylor's Big Band. In the years that followed, Coleman was heavily influenced by the music and rhythms of Cuba, Latin America, and West Africa.

Coleman's work with Taylor and other jazz professionals did not pay much, so he often performed on street corners and solicited tips from passersby. In the late 1980s, Coleman put together a street band with trumpeter Graham Haynes. The loosely knit group eventually evolved into the M-Base Collective, which had a revolving cast of more than sixty different members over the years. M-Base alumni include saxophonist Branford Marsalis, bassist Meshell N'degecello, pianist Geri Allen, and renowned jazz singer Cassandra Wilson.

M-Base stands for "Macro-Basic Array of Structured Extemporization." Extemporization means ad-libbing or improvisation. The collective's musicians were raised on jazz, rock, hip-hop, soul, and funk. Their music has been described as Motown soul with an irregular rhythm or meter.

Jazz Goes Digital

Musician and jazz critic Ted Gioia describes how computers, digital recording devices, and the Internet have transformed jazz music:

> The ways this technological revolution is impacting jazz are both subtle and profound. . . . At the Punkt Jazz Festival in Norway, audience members can go to the Alpha Room immediately after a concert and experience a "live" remix of the music they just heard—with DJs and guest musicians reworking the songs assisted by a stage full of equipment; indeed the remix is the heart of the festival, and often more exciting than the initial performance. Back in the States, trumpeter Dave Douglas performs in a jazz club, and a few hours later, is selling downloads of the music on his website. . . . [In] 2007 Dave Brubeck pulled off a "live" performance with the BBC Orchestra during which the pianist was in a studio in Rockefeller Plaza in New York, while the orchestra and conductor were facing the audience in London. . . . In North Carolina, a startup company called Zenph Studios is producing jazz recordings without any musicians at all, creating software equivalents of great performances of the past, virtual pianists and virtual bassists that are essentially indistinguishable from the originals.

Ted Gioia. *The History of Jazz*. New York: Oxford University Press, 2011, p. 370.

The Nature of the Universe

Coleman was inspired to produce music with a constantly changing meter while practicing outdoors in a park. He watched some bees fly by and was fascinated by the rotation of their wings and the organized flight patterns they took while swarming. Moved by nature's rhythmic models, Coleman said he began playing "within interwoven cyclical structures."[70]

Within the structure of the M-Base Collective, the intertwined meters occurred when the saxophone, piano, and rhythm section play simultaneously in different time signatures. This can be heard on the M-Base Collective 1992 album, *Anatomy of a Groove*. Coleman describes the album's sound as a "concept of improvisation . . . based on ideas about how to create music from one's experiences."[71]

After the album was released, Coleman journeyed to Ghana on the first of his many international musical research trips. Later journeys took him to Cuba, Senegal, and other places where he studied indigenous rhythms and melodies. Inspired by this wide variety of world music, Coleman adapted the sounds to fit within the jams of the M-Base Collective.

The term M-Base has come to define a jazz style that employs polymetry, or many meters, but Coleman never called the music itself M-Base. He considers M-Base to be a way of

Steve Coleman, performing at the 2011 Newport Jazz Festival, created the nu jazz sounds in the late 1980s.

life, rather than a music style. He says M-Base is a symbolic language "for expressing the nature of the universe—a force that sends out consciousness-expanding vibrations."[72]

Coleman continues to perform with his band Five Elements and uses his website (www.m-base.com) as a forum for his various musical projects. His site also provides free downloads of songs from his twenty-four albums. When asked why he gives his music away, Coleman responded, "My reasons for providing free music come from my belief that musical ideas should not be owned by anyone. I believe that ideas should be free for anyone to use."[73]

The Digital Sonic Doo-Bop

Coleman's sound is largely generated by traditional instruments, but in the 1990s countless jazz musicians incorporated high-tech gadgets into their acts. Computers and other digital tools increased in power, dropped in price, and changed the way people created music. By the end of the decade, a laptop computer was just as likely to be seen on a jazz stage as a saxophone.

Technological tools are used to manipulate traditional musical sounds or invent entirely new ones. Digital drum machines imitate the sounds of percussion instruments and can be programmed to create repetitive rhythm tracks. Music sequencers are sound manipulation programs that allow users to record, edit, alter, and play back music in many ways. Sampling software allows musicians to add prerecorded digitized snippets, or "samples," of music loops to their overall sound. These tools are at the heart of hip-hop production and new music genres that emerged in the 1990s such as electronica dance, house, and techno. British jazz critic Stuart Nicholson describes the role of digital tools in jazz: "Now the improviser's art can be played out against a new sonic backdrop colored by fragments of electronic sounds, rhythms, and samples swimming through the music."[74]

Samplers and other electronics are central to jazz rap. This style combines the rap and rhythms of hip-hop music with hot jazz licks. As jazz rap developed, Miles Davis once again led the way. Davis died in 1991, but in the last year of his life, he was inspired to make a jazz rap album while sitting in his New York apartment listening to sounds wafting up from the streets. Working with producer Easy Mo Bee, Davis played his smooth, iconic trumpet on a half dozen cool, jazzy songs. Mo Bee took some of the trumpet tracks, sampled and remixed them, and added hip-hop beats. On several songs he rapped over the hybridized music. The result was Davis's posthumous album *Doo-Bop,* released in 1992. The innovative album won a Grammy for Best R&B Instrumental Performance.

The Rebirth of Slick

Inspired by Davis's jazz rap, the hip-hop trio Digable Planets broke new ground with its 1993 album *Reachin' (A New Refutation of Time and Space).* It was not the lyrical content, but the album's musical background that made *Reachin'* stand out. The sounds are samples of jazz greats like Art Blakey, Herbie Hancock, Sonny Rollins, and others. *Reachin'* produced a surprise hit single, "Rebirth of Slick (Cool Like Dat)," a play on the Miles Davis title, *Birth of the Cool.* "Rebirth of Slick" peaked at number fifteen on the *Billboard* Hot 100 and won Digable Planets a Grammy Award for Rap Performance by a Group.

The publicity spawned by Digable Planets put jazz rap on the mainstream radar and helped the band Us3 achieve fame in 1994. Us3 was a London-based group founded by jazz writer Geoff Wilkinson and musician Mel Simpson. Wilkinson and Simpson hired rappers Kobie Powell, Rahsaan Kelly, and Tukka Yoot to make an album that fused hip-hop with classic jazz. The effort was given a boost when executives at the respected jazz label Blue Note Records allowed Us3 to sample from its catalog. The resulting album, *Hand on the Torch,* consists of catchy raps layered over the timeless licks of Horace Silver, Herbie Hancock, and Art Blakey. The single "Cantaloop (Flip Fantasia)" achieved gold status, selling more than 500,000 copies internationally.

Jazz rap also provided inspiration for A Tribe Called Quest and The Roots in the 1990s. The style was kept alive in the 2000s by rapper Guru, a member of the hip-hop group Gang Starr. Guru pursued a solo career with a four-volume series of albums called *Guru's Jazzmatazz*. The albums used live backing bands made up of jazz masters including Branford Marsalis, Hancock, trumpeters Donald Byrd and Freddie Hubbard, pianist Sonny Liston Smith, vocalist N'Dea Davenport, and dozens of others. The jazz bands are overlaid with hip-hop verses and samples from popular R&B and soul records. The last of the series, *Jazzmatazz, Vol. 4,* was released in 2007. Guru, whose real name was Keith Edward Elam, died of cancer in 2010 at the age of forty-eight.

Acid Jazz

Hip-hop rhythms played a major role in another evolving style known as acid jazz. The term is used to describe multistylistic music that combines soul, rap, pop, jazz, and electronica. The music can be diverse, combining everything from cool jazz to heavy fusion, but it is first and foremost dance music. This helped popularize acid jazz in European dance clubs during the past several decades.

Acid jazz can trace its roots to DJs in the 1980s who used old bebop and hard bop records to scratch on their turntables. Because these records were most often sold out of crates in used record stores, the DJs came to be known as rare groove crate diggers. Many jazz fans rejected the idea of a turntable as a musical instrument. However, the scratching sound produced by moving a record back and forth by hand can make a unique rhythmic groove. In 1983, Hancock was the first jazz musician to make a record with scratching, featuring the sound on his hit single "Rockit" from the album *Future Shock.*

The term acid jazz was coined in 1987 by a London DJ named Gilles Peterson who was searching for a term to define the diverse music he was hearing in dance clubs. During the 1990s, acid jazz was digitized by DJs who took jazz LPs from the 1950s and 1960s and created new sounds with sequencing, sampling, and looping. The resulting tracks were combined with percussion and electronic dance beats. This led to an evolution in the sound, which

James Taylor and Ivonne Yanney of James Taylor Quartet perform in 2011. The band was one of the first groups signed to British independent record label Acid Jazz.

was widely promoted by the British independent record label Acid Jazz.

Originally formed by Peterson in 1987, Acid Jazz was still active in the 2010s. Through the decades, the label has released dozens of albums made by groups that came out of the European club scene. The music includes a diverse blend

French Acid Jazz

Acid jazz has been popular in France for the past two decades. One of the leading purveyors of the sound, St. Germain, combines house and jazz styles into a unique blend of ethereal dance music. St. Germain, the stage name of producer Ludovic Navarre, released *Boulevard* in 1996. The record is a mixture of American R&B, jazz, and French synthesizer-based house music. *Boulevard* was one of the most popular acid jazz records of the 1990s, selling more than 350,000 copies.

St. Germain's second album, *Tourist* (2000), mixes electronics, jazz, blues, and funk samples with a live jazz band. Reviewer Andy Hermann calls the sound "Navarre's dreamy, down-tempo blend of dancefloor beats and cool-cat musicianship." *Tourist* was a worldwide hit, selling more than 4 million copies. St. Germain's success paved the way for other so-called "French touch" acid jazz artists such as Grand Tourism and Air.

Another French group, NoJazz, covers a dizzying diversity of styles. The group's 2000 single, "Freedom," is hyphenated jazz in an extreme form. The song might be described as hip-hop-bebop-fusion-electronica-Afro-Cuban-funk. The 2002 song "Boogaloo" cycles through funky swing and rap mixed with long jazzy big-band arrangements from the early 1960s.

of hyphenated jazz, funk, Latin, reggae, poetry, and what the label calls street-soul. Many leading acid jazz groups of the 1990s and 2000s recorded for the label, including Galliano, Chris Bangs, The Night Trains, The Last Poets, A Man Called Adam, and Snowboy & The Latin Section. Acid Jazz also produced annual compilation albums with various artists along with specialty albums such as *The History of Acid Jazz, Acid Jazz Rarities,* and *Smooth Acid Jazz,* all released in 2000.

The James Taylor Quartet was one of the first groups

signed by Acid Jazz, and it produced a wide range of sounds. On the 1996 album *A Few Useful Tips About Living Underground,* Taylor lays out funky and soulful jazz sounds on his Hammond organ while band members provide an assortment of various sounds. These include John McLaughlin–style fusion guitar, polished brass arrangements that sound like movie sound tracks, bubbling Cuban conga rhythms, and 1980s synthesizer sounds.

Jazz in Neverland

In the 2000s, acid jazz remained popular in Europe through groups such as the French band NoJazz and the German group Joo Kraus & Tales In Tones Trio. Kraus created an acid jazz remake of superstar Michael Jackson's biggest hits on the 2010 album *Songs From Neverland.* The *Neverland* remixes demonstrate that a wide range of sounds may be covered under the acid jazz title. Since the early 2000s, the sound has expanded beyond European borders to include Japanese artists such as DJ Krush and Gota and the Moscow Grooves Institute from Russia.

While many groups specialize in producing new sounds of acid jazz, several record labels have discovered the commercial potential of remixed jazz classics. In the 2000s, a number of compilations were produced with songs by Hancock, Airto, Davis, jazz guitarist George Benson, and others cut up, sampled, scratched, and looped to create songs for dance clubs. This phenomenon irritated musicians such as drummer Rashied Ali, who complains, "It's as if they were rewriting the Bible. This kind of remixing is the same thing as blasphemy."[75] Whatever the case, the beat-heavy droning jazz tracks were extremely popular with dancers and kept acid jazz alive as a distinctive style.

Diana Krall's Traditions

Despite the success of digital nu jazz, a few mainstream artists, such as Harry Connick Jr. and Diana Krall, have managed to keep the old musical traditions alive and produce best-selling jazz albums throughout the 1990s and 2000s.

Harry Connick Jr.

The pianist, composer, singer, and conductor Harry Connick Jr. is one of the most well-known jazz musicians of the twenty-first century. Born in New Orleans in 1967, Connick learned to play keyboards at the age of three and made his first jazz recordings when he was ten. Connick achieved widespread recognition for his second album *20*, so named because it was made when he was twenty years old. The album features show tunes and jazz standards like "Basin Street Blues."

Connick's mature singing style recalled Frank Sinatra from his big-band days and the young singer followed Sinatra's career path. Connick not only released big-band jazz albums but, like Sinatra, he made pop records and starred in blockbuster Hollywood movies. Throughout the 1990s, when not appearing in films like *Independence Day* and *Hope Floats*, Connick recorded a string of platinum-selling jazz albums including *Blue Light, Red Light*, *25*, and *Other Hours: Connick on Piano Volume 1*.

In the 2000s, Connick appeared in TV sitcoms, documentaries, and Broadway plays while continuing to record gold and platinum albums. By 2010, Connick had more than seven top-twenty albums, ten number-one jazz albums, and sold more than 16 million records. This placed Connick among the top sixty best-selling male artists in the United States.

Harry Connick Jr., one of the most popular jazz musicians of the twenty-first century, performs in New York City in 2010.

Pianist, singer, and composer Krall has had phenomenal success drawing from the jazz singers of the 1950s. Krall's free-flowing piano solos, sturdy alto voice, and traditional jazz arrangements made her an international star. Her 1999 album *When I Look in Your Eyes* earned her a Grammy for Best Jazz Vocal Performance. *When I Look in Your Eyes* was also the first jazz album to be nominated Album of the Year in twenty-five years.

Diana Krall sold more albums than any other female jazz artist in the 1990s and 2000s.

Krall was born in British Columbia, Canada, in 1964. She learned to play piano at the age of four and played her first jazz gig when she was fifteen. Krall's first album, *Stepping Out* (1993), was recorded with a simple jazz trio. She sings and tickles out the jazz melodies on the piano on standards such as "On the Sunny Side of the Street" and "Body and Soul" backed by a simple bass and drum combo. The album recalls classic Ella Fitzgerald, but Krall has her own unique voice, timing, and tone. On her second album, *Only Trust Your Heart* (1995), Krall adds some swinging brass but sticks with the jazz classics her great-grandparents likely danced to, such as Ellington's "Squeeze Me."

Krall married rock singer and songwriter Elvis Costello in 2003. The couple spent their first months together writing songs with Costello on lyrics and Krall composing melodies. Their work was released on the 2004 album *The Girl in the Other Room*. The spare arrangements, slow bluesy tempos, and sultry vocals that dominate the album invoke the spirit of 1950s–era jazz singer Peggy Lee. *The Girl in the Other Room* peaked at number four on the *Billboard* 200 pop charts.

Krall's appropriately titled *Quiet Nights,* released in 2009, continued her string of slow, mellow, jazzy albums that evoke visions of smoky nightclubs at 3 A.M. *Quiet Nights* reached number three on the pop charts and number one on the jazz charts. By 2011, Krall had sold more than 15 million records worldwide, more than any other female jazz artist of the 1990s and 2000s. By that time, she had also won three Grammys, eight Canadian Juno Awards, and was the only female singer to have eight jazz albums debut at number one on the *Billboard* Jazz Albums chart.

Esperanza Spalding Is Wild as the Wind

While Krall's style remained tied to traditional jazz, bassist Esperanza Spalding began making headlines in the 2000s as a true jazz original. She took her inspirations from hip-hop, alternative rock, blues, funk, and fusion, as well as Brazilian and Cuban styles. Born in Portland, Oregon, in 1984, Spalding was only five when she taught herself to play the violin. She also learned the oboe and clarinet before she was nine and picked up the string bass at the age of fifteen. After learning a few blues licks on the bass, she fell in love with the instrument and began playing it on a daily basis.

Spalding attended the Berklee College of Music where she had a life-changing conversation with Pat Metheny,

Jazz original Esperanza Spalding plays a mix of free jazz and Latin music with scat vocals.

who was visiting the school to produce a record by the student ensemble. Spalding describes the encounter:

> Everybody had left the studio and I was there, probably practicing and Mr. Metheny walked in and asked me what I was planning to do with my life. I told him that I was thinking of leaving school and pursuing a degree in political science. He told me that he meets a lot of musicians, some great, some not so great and that I had (what he called) the "X Factor." Meaning, that if I chose to pursue a career in music and I applied myself, my potential was unlimited.[76]

Spalding took Metheny's advice and became a professional musician. Before she was twenty, she played with jazz greats such as saxophonist Joe Lovano, vocalist Patti Austin, and Metheny himself. In 2005, she formed her own acoustic jazz trio and started a solo career, releasing her debut album *Junjo* the following year. Spalding co-wrote three of the nine songs on the album, and the overall sound is a hybrid of free jazz and Latin played with an irresistible syncopation. Spalding's fingers dance and fly across the bass neck, and her playful scat vocals bring forth imagery of beatniks singing in coffeehouses in the early 1960s.

A Genre unto Itself

Spalding wrote or co-wrote all but two of the songs on her 2010 Grammy-winning album *Chamber Music Society*. This record shows off Spalding's talents, not only as a bassist but as an ambitious composer, arranger, and producer. The album touches on a wide range of sounds, which serve as a canvas for Spalding's lithe singing and finger-popping bass runs. The song "Chacarera" features a syncopated Latin groove, while "Wild Is the Wind" is a slow tango that builds with dramatic intensity along with Spalding's vocals. "Knowledge of Good and Evil" has a slight sonic dissonance and melodic harmony with roots in the early 1970s fusion of Weather Report.

In 2010, Spalding was promoting jazz to mainstream audiences on TV and radio, in concert, and on the Web. She appeared on the *Oprah Winfrey Show,* the *David Letterman*

Show, and even played for President Barack Obama. Her future plans include an album titled *Radio Music Society*, which promises to combine funk, hip-hop, and rock elements into a Spaldingesque jazz sound. Spalding's music seems to be a genre unto itself, and perhaps someday historians will write about the Spalding style of jazz as much as they focus on bebop or swing today.

As Spalding demonstrates, jazz music, in all of its various forms, remains alive for its fans. Even though jazz records only made up 4 to 5 percent of all CD sales worldwide in 2010, the music is firmly established as an integral part of American culture and history. The musical style first played by Buddy Bolden during the early 1900s has traveled a long and illustrious path, and its impact upon twenty-first century American music is undisputed. With albums such as Miles Davis's 1959 *Kind of Blue* still selling around 250,000 copies a year, there is little doubt that the sounds of jazz will continue to resonate for generations to come.

NOTES

Introduction: "Never Played the Same Way Once"

1. Joachim-Ernst Berendt and Günther Huesmann. *The Jazz Book: From Ragtime to the 21st Century.* Chicago: Lawrence Hill Books, 2009, p. 1.
2. Quoted in Bill Crow. *Jazz Anecdotes: Second Time Around.* New York: Oxford University Press, 2005, p. 21.
3. Quoted in Public Broadcasting Service. "Classroom." *Jazz: A Film by Ken Burns.* PBS, 2011. www.pbs.org.

Chapter 1: The Roots of Jazz

4. Quoted in John Edward Hasse, ed. *Jazz: The First Century.* New York: William Morrow, 2000, p. 5.
5. Mark C. Gridley. *Jazz Styles: History and Analysis.* Englewood Cliffs, NJ: Prentice Hall, 1988, p. 40.
6. Berendt and Huesmann. *The Jazz Book*, p. 5.
7. Clyde E.B. Bernhardt. *I Remember: Eighty Years of Black Entertainment, Big Bands, and the Blues.* Philadelphia: University of Pennsylvania Press, 1986, p. 7.

8. Hasse. *Jazz: The First Century*, p. 16.
9. Quoted in Alyn Shipton. *A New History of Jazz.* New York: Continuum, 2001, p. 84.
10. Shipton. *A New History of Jazz*, p. 82.
11. Quoted in Berendt and Huesmann. *The Jazz Book*, p. 6.
12. Quoted in Berendt and Huesmann. *The Jazz Book*, p. 6.
13. Quoted in Crow. *Jazz Anecdotes*, p. 120.
14. Quoted in Hasse. *Jazz: The First Century*, p. 17.
15. Quoted in Hasse. *Jazz: The First Century*, p. 18.
16. Quoted in Shipton. *A New History of Jazz*, p. 96.

Chapter 2: Swingin' Jazz Bands

17. Quoted in George E. Mowry. *The Twenties: Fords, Flappers & Fanatics.* Englewood Cliffs, NJ: Prentice-Hall, 1963, p. 66.
18. Shipton. *A New History of Jazz*, p. 138.
19. Quoted in Geoffrey C. Ward. *Jazz: A Film by Ken Burns, Episode 2: The Gift.* Florentine Films, 2000.

20. Edward Kennedy "Duke" Ellington. *Music Is My Mistress*. Doubleday & Company, 1973, p. 106.
21. Quoted in Geoffrey C. Ward. *Jazz: A Film by Ken Burns, Episode 4: The True Welcome*. Florentine Films, 2000.
22. Hasse. *Jazz: The First Century*, p. 54.
23. Quoted in Ward. *Jazz: A Film by Ken Burns, Episode 4: The True Welcome*.
24. Quoted in Ward. *Jazz: A Film by Ken Burns, Episode 4: The True Welcome*.
25. Quoted in Shipton. *A New History of Jazz*, p. 308.
26. Quoted in Shipton. *A New History of Jazz*, p. 325.

Chapter 3: The Birth of Bebop

27. Quoted in Ted Gioia. *The History of Jazz*. New York: Oxford University Press, 2011, p. 201.
28. Quoted in Gioia. *The History of Jazz*, p. 256.
29. Quoted in Kenny Mathieson. *Giant Steps: Bebop and the Creators of Modern Jazz, 1945–65*. Edinburgh, Scotland: Payback Press, 1999, p. 7.
30. Quoted in Scott DeVeaux. *The Birth of Bebop*. Berkeley: University of California Press, 1997, p. 218.
31. Quoted in Shipton. *A New History of Jazz*, p. 444.
32. Gridley. *Jazz Styles: History and Analysis*, pp. 152–153.
33. Dizzy Gillespie and Al Fraser. *To Be, or Not . . . to Bop*. Garden City, NY: Doubleday, 1979, p. 318.
34. Quoted in Geoffrey C. Ward. *Jazz: A Film by Ken Burns, Episode 8: Risk*. Florentine Films, 2000.
35. Mathieson. *Giant Steps*, p. 160
36. Quoted in Shipton. *A New History of Jazz*, p. 484.
37. Quoted in DeVeaux. *The Birth of Bebop*, p. 222.

Chapter 4: The Cool and the Hard

38. Berendt and Huesmann. *The Jazz Book*, p. 16.
39. Quoted in Gioia. *The History of Jazz*, p. 253.
40. Quoted in Ward. *Jazz: A Film by Ken Burns, Episode 8: Risk*.
41. Quoted in Frank Alkyer, ed. *The Miles Davis Reader*. New York: Hal Leonard Books, 2007, p. 66.
42. Geoffrey C. Ward. *Jazz: A History of America's Music*. New York: Alfred A. Knopf, 2000, p. 375.
43. Quoted in Shipton. *A New History of Jazz*, p. 701.
44. Quoted in Shipton. *A New History of Jazz*, p. 702.
45. Quoted in Ward. *Jazz: A History of America's Music*, p. 378.
46. Quoted in Hasse. *Jazz: The First Century*, p. 115.
47. Gridley. *Jazz Styles: History and Analysis*, p. 191.
48. Hasse. *Jazz: The First Century*, p. 116.

49. Quoted in Shipton. *A New History of Jazz*, p. 673.
50. Carl Woideck, ed. *The John Coltrane Companion*. New York: Schirmer Books, 1998, p. xiii.
51. Quoted in Woideck. *The John Coltrane Companion*, p. 34.
52. Quoted in Shipton. *A New History of Jazz*, p. 746.
53. Quoted in Geoffrey C. Ward. *Jazz: A Film by Ken Burns, Episode 9: The Adventure*. Florentine Films, 2000.
54. Gioia. *The History of Jazz*, p. 253.

Chapter 5: Free Jazz and Fusion

55. Gridley. *Jazz Styles: History and Analysis*, p. 227.
56. Gioia. *The History of Jazz*, p. 315.
57. Quoted in Berendt and Huesmann. *The Jazz Book*, p. 379.
58. Dirk Sutro. *Jazz for Dummies*. Foster City, CA: IDG Books Worldwide, 1998, pp. 243–244.
59. Quoted in Bill Kirchner, ed. *The Oxford Companion to Jazz*. Oxford, England: Oxford University Press, 2000, p. 489.
60. Quoted in Gioia. *The History of Jazz*, p. 311.
61. Quoted in Shipton. *A New History of Jazz*, p. 856.
62. Quoted in Kirchner. *The Oxford Companion to Jazz*, p. 505.
63. Quoted in Kirchner. *The Oxford Companion to Jazz*, p. 503.
64. Quoted in Kirchner. *The Oxford Companion to Jazz*, p. 502.
65. Gridley. *Jazz Styles: History and Analysis*, p. 326.
66. Quoted in Hasse. *Jazz: The First Century*, p. 198.
67. Quoted in Hasse. *Jazz: The First Century*, p. 200.

Chapter 6: Nu Jazz for New Times

68. Quoted in Berendt and Huesmann. *The Jazz Book*, p. 44.
69. Quoted in Berendt and Huesmann. *The Jazz Book*, p. 43.
70. Quoted in Berendt and Huesmann. *The Jazz Book*, p. 71.
71. Steve Coleman. "Bio." M-Base.com, 2011. www.m-base.com/resume_bio.html.
72. Quoted in Berendt and Huesmann. *The Jazz Book*, p. 71.
73. Steve Coleman. "Why Do I Give Away Some of My Music." M-base.com, 2011. www.m-base.com/give_away.html.
74. Quoted in Berendt and Huesmann. *The Jazz Book*, p. 67.
75. Quoted in Berendt and Huesmann. *The Jazz Book*, p. 70.
76. Quoted in Tomas Peña. "In Conversation with Esperanza Spalding." Jazz.com, June 13, 2008. www.jazz.com.

Louis Armstrong

Armstrong Plays W.C. Handy, 1954

Satchmo's interpretations of Handy's hits such as "Beale Street Blues" and "St. Louis Blues" make this album a jazz classic and one of Armstrong's best-sellers of the 1950s.

The Complete Hot Five and Hot Seven Recordings, 2000

Armstrong's sound on this collection of songs was so new, complex, and rich that no one had ever heard anything like it before. While the poor sound quality takes some getting used to, this is Armstrong in his prime, making jazz history with some of the best musicians of the era.

Chet Baker

Chet, 1959

Baker records the coolest of West Coast cool with an all-star lineup that includes Pepper Adams, Herbie Mann, Kenny Burrell, and Connie Kay.

Count Basie

Count Basie at Newport, 1957

The Complete Decca Recordings (1937–1939), 1992

This three-disc set of classics with Lester Young, Buck Clayton, and singer Jimmy Rushing, among others, presents Basie during his glory days. A close listen can reveal sounds of boogie-woogie and rock and roll yet to come. In addition, considering the songs were recorded more than seven decades ago, the sound quality is impeccable.

Sidney Bechet

16 Classic Performances, 2005

The title says it all. These are not simply songs but exciting performances that feature the singular sax and clarinet soloist at his swinging, swooping, and swaying best.

Art Blakey

At the Café Bohemia, 1955

The Jazz Messengers, 1956

Art Blakey's Jazz Messengers With Thelonious Monk, 1958

Dave Brubeck

Jazz at Oberlin, 1953

Time Out (50th Anniversary Legacy Edition), 2009

Brubeck's cool jazz experiment with various time signatures made him a household name, a rarity even in the 1950s. This edition is a remastered version of the classic album that features "Take Five" and includes early 1960s live versions of various songs.

Ornette Coleman

Free Jazz: A Collective Improvisation, 1961

Coleman officially launched the free jazz movement with this controversial and often painfully dissonant record. One thirty-seven-minute track takes up the entire two sides of the album, and the right and left channels of stereo feature separate performance by two different quartets playing improvised music.

John Coltrane

Blue Trane, 1957

Giant Steps, 1960

Coltrane's first album of all original compositions, this record blasts off with "Giant Steps" and it seems as if the sax master hardly takes a breath until the album winds up seven songs later with "Mr. P.C." This album lets listeners hear why Coltrane's music is described as "sheets of sound."

Ascension, 1966

Harry Connick Jr.

25, 1992

30, 2001

Chanson du Vieux Carré, 2007

Most of Connick's late 2000s albums consist of pop standards, Broadway show tunes, and Christmas songs. On this album, Connick performs original, mostly instrumental, jazz tracks with a big band.

Chick Corea

Return to Forever, 1972

Corea's legendary lineup, which includes Stanley Clarke, Airto Moreira, and Flora Purim, melds psychedelic space music, fusion, Latin, Brazilian, and a few other styles into a sound that remains fresh decades after it was recorded.

Miles Davis

Bags' Groove, 1954

Kind of Blue, 1959

Miles Smiles, 1966

Bitches Brew, 1970

The Complete Birth of the Cool, 1998

This remastered double-disc contains the entire twelve-track album released by Capitol Records in 1957 along with three 1948 radio broadcasts performed by the Miles Davis Nonet. These historic recordings provide an essential introduction to Davis and the cool sound he pioneered.

Digable Planets

Reachin' (A New Refutation of Time and Space), 1993

Duke Ellington

70th Birthday Concert, 1969

Cotton Club Days, 2008

Duke Ellington and John Coltrane

Duke Ellington & John Coltrane, 1962

Two of history's most revered jazz musicians meet on an album of seven sophisticated songs.

Duke Ellington and Louis Armstrong

The Great Summit—Complete Sessions, 2000

Ella Fitzgerald

Ella Fitzgerald Sings the Duke Ellington Songbook, 1957

Ella not only shows off her matchless jazz chops singing Ellington, she does it with Duke and his orchestra. Ellington was even inspired to compose a few songs specifically for this album including the sixteen-minute "Portrait of Ella Fitzgerald" and the swinging "E and D Blues."

Ella Fitzgerald and Louis Armstrong

Ella and Louis, 1957

Dizzy Gillespie

Live At Massey Hall, 1953, 1953

Dizzy blows the bop with Bud Powell, Charles Mingus, and Max Roach, kicking out the polyrhythms to a cheering crowd on "A Night in Tunisia," "Perdido," and "Salt Peanuts."

The Complete RCA Victor Recordings, 1995

Benny Goodman

Centennial Celebration, 1965

The Complete RCA Victor Small Group Recordings, 1997

Live at Carnegie Hall—1938 Complete, 1999

The January night Goodman took his big band to the world's most respected classical music venue is considered one of the most important nights in jazz. Songs on this three-disc set from the vintage 1950 recording feature superstars Count Basie, Gene Krupa, Lionel Hampton, Cootie Williams, Lester Young, and Buck Clayton kicking it out at Carnegie.

Guru

Jazzmatazz, Volumes 1–4, 1993–2007

Herbie Hancock

Head Hunters, 1973

Hancock melds jazz fusion and electronic music using an early synthesizer to create shrieking funk and tribal jam beats.

Coleman Hawkins

Body and Soul, 1988

Songs of the sax master recorded between 1939 and 1956.

The Essential Sides Remastered 1929–1933, 2006

The Essential Sides Remastered 1934–1936, 2006

Billie Holiday

The Complete Billie Holiday on Columbia 1933–1944, 2001

The definitive collection, ten discs of Lady Day in her prime, backed by Basie, Goodman, Lester Young, Teddy Wilson, and other greats, featuring classics such as "God Bless the Child," "Am I Blue?," and "Strange Fruit."

James Taylor Quartet

A Few Useful Tips About Living Underground, 1996

On this acid jazz classic, organist and arranger Taylor brings together perky 1960s movie sound track brass, a 1970s fusion style reminiscent of Mahavishnu Orchestra, and 1980s jazz funk.

Freddie Keppard

Freddie Keppard—The Complete Set (1923–1926), 2000

Kid Ory

Kid Ory, 2004

Diana Krall

Stepping Out, 1993

Quiet Nights, 2009

Wynton Marsalis

Wynton Marsalis, 1981

Marsalis not only reinvented hard bop as neo-bop on this album, he did so with Miles Davis's legendary band, Herbie Hancock, Ron Carter, and Tony Williams. Listening to this disc, it is easy to understand why jazz critics were praising the astoundingly talented nineteen-year-old trumpeter as the 1980s savior of true jazz.

M-Base Collective

Anatomy of a Groove, 1992

John McLaughlin and the Mahavishnu Orchestra

Birds of Fire, 1973

Glenn Miller

Golden Years: 1938–1942, 2001

Charles Mingus

Mingus Ah Um, 1959

Mingus, Mingus, Mingus, Mingus, Mingus, 1963

Passions of a Man: The Complete Atlantic Recordings, 1956–1961, 1997

Thelonious Monk

Monk's Dream, 1963

The Complete Blue Note Recordings, 1994

On these four discs, recorded between 1947 and 1952 with Sonny Rollins, Art Blakey, Max Roach, and other luminaries, Monk shows off his quirky improvisational style and songwriting chops. Signature compositions include "Ruby My Dear," "Misterioso," and "Straight, No Chaser."

Gerry Mulligan

The Original Quartet With Chet Baker, 1998

Charlie Parker

Yardbird Suite: The Ultimate Collection, 1997

On these thirty-eight tracks taken from Parker's most creative period, listeners can hear Bird's astonishing phrasing, virtuosity, speed, and improvisations on timeless classics such as "Night in Tunisia," "Parker's Mood," and "Ko Ko."

Charlie Parker and Dizzy Gillespie

Bird & Diz, 1956

Historic sounds by the legendary godfathers of bebop, with Thelonious Monk on piano, burn through "Bloomdido," "Leapfrog," "Mohawk," and others, with multiple takes of every song.

The Pat Metheny Group

American Garage, 1980

Metheny's guitar jazz fusion, in all its 1980s phase-shifting glory, features Lyle Mays on keys, Mark Egan on bass, and the inimitable Danny Gottlieb on drums.

Esperanza Spalding

Junjo, 2006

Esperanza, 2008

Chamber Music Society, 2010

The album that helped Spalding beat out Justin Bieber for a Grammy and put jazz and—perhaps most unlikely—the doghouse bass, at the forefront of modern music. Even die-hard rock and pop fans can find something to love on this album because Spalding's compositions, arrangements, singing, and instrumental voicings are as unique as a jazz giant from any era.

Cecil Taylor

Air, 1960

Unit Structures, 1966

Us3

Hand on the Torch, 1993

Various Artists

Nu Jazz Anthology, 2010

Weather Report

Weather Report, 1971

Heavy Weather, 1977

Lester Young

Lester Young With the Oscar Peterson Trio, 1952

Listening to Lester weave and dodge around the melodies, listeners can understand why he was called the "President" or the "Prez" and credited with inventing modern jazz.

The Basics, 2011

This iTunes Essentials compilation features the "Prez" jumpin' and jivin' with Basie, Billie Holiday, the Kansas City Five, and others.

GLOSSARY

album: Originally used to describe a 12-inch (30 cm) vinyl, long-playing (LP) record that played at 33 rpm (revolutions per minute) and could hold about twenty minutes of music on each side. In the digital age, an album is any collection of songs released together by an artist.

boogie-woogie: A fast-tempo, swinging, or shuffling rhythm used in jazz, rock, and other pop music styles.

chops: Musical skills. A player with good chops has the ability to create exciting improvised musical passages on an instrument.

chord: A set of notes played on an instrument simultaneously.

crescendo: Music played increasingly loud or intensely; the musical climax of a song.

diatonic: The traditional seven-note musical scale, sung as do-re-me-fa-so-la-ti.

improvisation: The act of creating music on the spot.

meter: The pattern of rhythm within music.

polyrhythm: The simultaneous playing of two or more independent rhythms, which gives music a danceable momentum.

scat singing: A series of nonsensical words or sounds most often meant to imitate the snarling sounds of a trumpet.

single: Originally, any record with one song on each side. Originally, singles were sold as 7-inch (17.7 cm) vinyl records that played at 45 rpm (revolutions per minute). In the digital age, a single is any one song that is promoted separately from an album.

syncopation: A rhythm style in which the drummer highlights the second and fourth beats, or "backbeats," in each four-beat measure.

synthesizer: An electronic instrument, usually played with a keyboard, that produces unique complex sounds or those that mimic other instruments such as violins and horns.

twelve-bar, or 12-bar: One of the most popular chord progressions in popular music with roots in the blues, wherein each verse occupies twelve bars, or measures, in musical notation.

vibrato: A throbbing effect in singing or on a musical instrument.

FOR MORE INFORMATION

Books

Stefan Berg. *Let That Bad Air Out: Buddy Bolden's Last Parade.* Erin, Ontario: Porcupine's Quill, 2007. This graphic novel tells the story of New Orleans jazz legend Buddy Bolden with dazzling images that evoke the rowdiness of his life, the volatility of his music, and the darkness of his mental demise.

Rodney P. Carlisle. *The Roaring Twenties: 1920 to 1929.* New York: Facts On File, 2009. This book explains the cultural, political, and social world of the Jazz Age with details about Prohibition, bootleggers, the Harlem Renaissance, and jazz music.

Forrest Cole. *Billie Holiday: Singer.* New York: Chelsea House, 2011. Lady Day's life was marked by pain and tragedy, which was only alleviated by singing. This biography covers the troubles faced by the legendary blues and jazz vocalist and the impact she made on the music world.

Carin T. Ford. *Duke Ellington: I Live with Music.* Berkeley Heights, NJ: Enslow, 2007. This biography provides details about the composer, bandleader, and pianist who topped all other jazz musicians of his day by infusing the rhythms of jazz with a classical, sophisticated sound.

Cicily Janus. *The New Face of Jazz: An Intimate Look at Today's Living Legends and the Artists of Tomorrow.* New York: Billboard Books, 2010. This illustrated compendium provides revealing details of many of today's shining stars of jazz. Each entry features a brief analysis, followed by the artist's own words describing his or her approach to music.

Ronnie D. Lankford. *Jazz.* Detroit: Gale Cengage Learning, 2011. This book puts the history of jazz in a musical and cultural context, covering the innovators and the prejudice they faced as they struggled to bring their songs to the world.

Kenneth Partridge. *Louis Armstrong: Musician.* New York: Chelsea House, 2011. This biography details the life of the greatest jazz innovator, tracing his journey from an impoverished childhood in New Orleans to his stunning musical accomplishments on the world stage.

Michael V. Uschan, ed. *The Blues.* Detroit: Gale Cengage Learning, 2011. The blues is the beating heart of jazz, rock, and pop music. This book covers the influential musical style from its nineteenth-century roots to its respected place among the musical canon of the twenty-first century.

Websites

All About Jazz (www.allaboutjazz.com). This comprehensive jazz website features up-to-date articles, album reviews, interviews, free MP3s, videos, photos, forums, guides, and concert calendars.

DownBeat (www.downbeat.com). *DownBeat* magazine, founded in 1937, remains the premier "book of record for the jazz world" in the twenty-first century. The magazine's website offers the latest news, record reviews, select articles from its archives, and digital subscriptions for access to the magazine's latest issues.

Jazz at Lincoln Center (www.jalc.org). This website, maintained by Lincoln Center in New York City, offers jazz songs, podcasts, jazz radio, music videos, concert footage, and an assortment of jazz education programs for young people and adults.

M-Base Collective (www.m-base.com). This site, maintained by virtuoso alto saxophonist Steve Coleman, explains the polymetry concept of the M-Base sound, lists the more than sixty players who have been in the collective, and provides free downloads of all Coleman's twenty-four albums recorded since the early 1990s.

Wynton Marsalis (http://wyntonmarsalis.com). In the twenty-first century, Marsalis is the leading jazz advocate and educator. His official website has the usual tour info, store, and biographical information but also includes an education section with videos of Marsalis's priceless master classes and music lessons.

Films

Bird, 2001
Jazz fan and movie star Clint Eastwood produced this moody, dark biopic with Forest Whittaker starring as Charlie "Yardbird" Parker. Although the movie dwells on Parker's heroin abuse, it also shows him as an eloquent and intelligent man boxed in by racism and an unenlightened listening public. Bird's music alone makes this film worth watching.

Dizzy Gillespie Live in '58 and '70, 2006
This DVD features two European concerts, one from 1958, the other from 1970, both showing Gillespie in fine form. The 1958 concert features Gillespie with a small combo. The 1970 show has Dizzy doubling as bandleader and soloist, leading a sixteen-piece big band that covers hard bop, funk, and bluesy grooves.

Jazz: A Film by Ken Burns, 2000
This love letter to jazz originally appeared in ten episodes on PBS. With great music by the masters and rare old film footage and photographs, the viewer not only learns about jazz music history, but also gets a taste and feel for the times, the lives of the musicians, and the overarching rac-

ism that many of the world's greatest players dealt with on a daily basis.

Lady Sings the Blues, 1972

Diana Ross stars as the legendary Billie Holiday in this biopic that chronicles Lady Day's rise to fame and her fall due to substance addictions. The film covers Holiday's late childhood, her time as a prostitute, her early singing days, the racism she faced, and her tragic later years. While the story strays from fact, Ross was deservedly nominated for an Oscar for her singing performances and realistic portrayal of this jazz great.

Louis Armstrong Live in '59, 2006

This hour-long DVD, originally filmed in Belgium, is the only complete Armstrong show known to exist. Although Satchmo's groundbreaking work was decades in the past, his chops had only improved over the years as his updated treatments of Dixieland standards like "St. Louis Blues" and "Hold That Tiger" attest.

Miles! Live at Montreux—The Definitive Miles Davis at Montreux Collection, 1973–1991, 2011

This ten-disc collection features every performance Davis gave at the world's premier jazz festival including the last one only three months before his death. While many songs are repeated, listeners can hear how the tunes evolved over the years and were "never played . . . the same way once."

INDEX

A

Acid jazz, 100–103
Air (band), 102
Ali, Rashied, 103
Alias, Don, 86
Allen, Geri, 95
Altissimo, 78
Ansermet, Ernest, 21–22
Armstrong, Louis, 8–9, 27–30, *27*, 34–35, 46–47, 56
Armstrong, Ralphe, *87*
Art Ensemble of Chicago, 78
Atonal dissonance, 79
Austin, Patti, 108

B

Baker, Chet, 65, 66, *66*, 67
Bangs, Chris, 102
Baquet, George, 21
Basie, William "Count," 34, 35, 40–41
Beatles, 65, 82, 83, 84
Bebop
　"bop prosody," 58
　chromatic scales and, 46
　development, 49–54
　diatonic scales and, 51
　flatted fifth, 51
　free jazz and, 79
　hard bop, 62, 68, 70–76
　hot jazz, 61
　improvisation and, 46, 47, 49
　musical instruments, 46
　neo-bop, 92, 93
　overview, 45–47
　polyrhythms, 46, 52, 61
Bechet, Sidney, 21–22, *22*
Benson, George, 103
Bent notes, 12, 74–75
Berigan, Bunny, 42
Berklee College of Music, 89, 106
Bernhardt, Clyde E.B., 15–16
Big-band jazz, 33–38
Blakey, Art, 70, *70*, 71, 99
Blood, Sweat & Tears, 83
Blue Note Records, 99
Blue notes, 8
Blues hollers, 12
Blues songs, 12–13, 16, 76, 79
Bolden, Charles "Buddy," 16–19, *17*, 25, 109
Boogie-woogie, 40, 41, 51, 79
Brackeen, JoAnne, 72
Brooks, Harvey, 86
Brown, Les, 44
Brubeck, Dave, 67–68, *68*, 76, 96
Burroughs, William, 58
Byrd, Donald, 72, 100
Byrds (band), 82

C

Call-and-response, 12, 13, 78–79
Calloway, Cab, 47, 51
Capitol Records, 64
Carter, Benny, 37, 44
Chicago style jazz, 30–31

Roberts, Marcus, 93
Robertson, Zue, 20
Rock and roll, 62, 65, 76, 83
Rodgers, Richard, 31
Rogers, Shorty, 66
Rolling Stones, 84, 87
Rollins, Sonny, 60, 71, 99
Roots, The (band), 99

S

Sampling, 98, 100
Savoy Ballroom (New York, NY), 31, *36*, 37
Scat singing, 29, 31, 108
Scott, Tony, 48
Scratching (of records), 100, 103
Shank, Bud, 66
Shaw, Artie, 35
Shaw, Woody, 72
Shorter, Wayne, 72, 86, 90
Shout vocals, 40–41
Silent spaces, 59
Silver, Horace, 71, 99
Simpson, Mel, 99
Sinatra, Frank, 36, 45, 104
Slang, 52, 60, 71
Smith, Sonny Liston, 100
Snowboy & The Latin Section, 102
Sophisticated jazz sound, 33, 34
Soul jazz, 76
Spalding, Esperanza, 6, 9, 106, *107*
Spirituals/gospel music, 12, 16, 76, 81
St. Germain (artist), 102
Stacey, Jess, 42
Stomp jazz, 41
Storyville district (New Orleans, LA), 11–12, 20, 28
Swing, 7–8, 23, 46, 47, 93
Syncopation, 7–8, 12, 13, 23, 108
Synthesizers, 84, 95, 102, 103

T

Taylor, Cecil, 78–79, *80*, 81–82, 95
Taylor, James, *101*
Teagarden, Jack, 30, 44
Technology and music, 84, 98–99
Thornhill, Claude, 62
Tribe Called Quest, 99
Tyner, McCoy, 91

U

Us3, 99

V

Vaughn, Sarah, 36, 45

W

Ward, Helen, 42, 44
Weather Report (band), 90
Webb, Chick, 31
West Coast jazz, 61, 65–67
White, Lenny, 86
White, Michael, 15
Wilkinson, Geoff, 99
Williams, Cootie, 37
Wilson, Cassandra, 95

Y

Yanney, Ivonne, *101*
Young, Lester, 35, 40, 47

Z

Zappa, Frank, 82
Zawinul, Joe, 86, 90–91

PICTURE CREDITS

ABOUT THE AUTHOR

Stuart A. Kallen is the author of more than 250 nonfiction books for children and young adults. He has written extensively about science, the environment, music, culture, history, and folklore. In addition, Mr. Kallen has written award-winning children's videos and television scripts. In his spare time, he is a singer/songwriter/guitarist in San Diego, California.